AF492554

The NEEDS of the HEART

PHILLIP ANDERSON

Copyright © 2019 by Phillip C. Anderson

All rights reserved. No part of this book may be reproduced or
used in any manner without written permission of the copyright
owner except for the use of quotations in a book review.

For more information, address: PhillipAnderson@books.com

FIRST EDITION

www.PhillipAndersonbooks.com

CONTENTS

INTRODUCTION

am not prone to dismiss logic, reason, strategy, or any other analytical processes of the left hemisphere of the human brain. However, I am a man who believes that there is more to life than just having one outlook. I am of the belief that emotions are just as powerful and just as necessary as logic, reason, and all the other rational approaches to life. I believe that what makes life grand is the emotional factor that comes with it. I would rather feel, experience, live in the moment, and have a genuine connection to that which I feel than to just view it from an analytical point of view. The best part of being human is that we have both options. We have the ability to live in the moment and connect on a deep level to the people, things, and experiences we encounter in our life. We can also cognitively approach something from afar while at the same time determining whether or not to attach ourselves to it. However, my main emphasis is the emotional connection we have to people. From our emotions comes the connections we forge, and from those connections come beautiful things. The human heart is one of the greatest things ever gifted to humanity; in our limited time on this earth (this physical realm), we can live and remember how we lived before we die. It is our emotions that give our memories that much more weight and depth rather than being only cognitive catalogs of what we experience. It is our emotions that allows us to interact in our environment and amongst others in a way that is more genuine than viewing life strictly from a logical and detached point of view. In my opinion, the essence of life is to be lived, and you can only live if you feel. It is only when you are in tune with your emotions that you truly draw breathe. It is only when you let your emotions flow through you that you open yourself to life and feel it.

It hurts to see people view emotions in such a negative fashion. That we can easily be deceived, manipulated, and even abused by our own emotions, does not make emotions a bad thing. It is not wrong to have a heart. It is not wrong to care. Love is something that is not for the weak. Regardless of the day and age, emotions are something that will always be misunderstood by most people. But that does not mean that emotions are ambiguous by nature. I see the human heart, human emotions as the greatest source of humanity's strength. For in the acceptance of such emotions comes the acceptance of the human soul. But I also see the downfall that is caused by their emotions due to the simple fact that very few take the time to understand themselves from an emotional point of view. I believe the understanding of human emotions goes farther than just emotional intelligence in the sense of how most people use and view them. We should try to understand, acceptance, and embrace each other, for our soul, for who we are and how our emotions relate to them specifically. Like all things that have latent power, potential, and greatness, the human heart is something that must be understood. Not just for a day, a month, a year, but until the end of our time. For the heart longs to be understood, and you start by understanding one's emotions. We must never forget that emotions in and of themselves are not the downfall of humanity; instead, Humanity's lack of eagerness to understand itself in its entirety is the reason for its downfall.

My father once told me that life is like a game of cards. He said that each person is dealt a different hand. Some people have the best hand that automatically puts them ahead at winning the game. Some people have a good enough hand where if they pick up a couple of more cards, they just might win the game. Some people just have nothing good going for them. Even if they continue to pick up more cards, it is not enough for them to win the game. Why do I tell you this? As it pertains to life, we each are born into different states. Some are born into wealth; others into generational wealth that dates back generations. Some are born into an okay standing where they have not too much and not too little in terms of economic goods and resources. And some are just dealt a horrible, born into terrible circumstances. With each level of the social ladder comes a different perspective on life, a different outlook on the same reality we all share. Yet we each have something to say about what we believe is true. We each see something that the other does not and seek to expand upon it. As each person strives for what they desire, they give up something else to achieve their goal. We all give up our soul to advance ourselves in the eyes of others. We give up the things that matter the most but that we think don't matter at the time. Looking back, we realize that we had all we ever needed, we just didn't know it. We accept pragmatism, logic, reasoning, strategy, and all the other cognitive ingredients we tell ourselves will make the most sense to achieve our dreams, but most times we do so at the costs of our souls. We give up the idealistic and childlike nature we once had to grow up and make this world a better place (by our own accounts). Is this wrong? Idealism alone is not enough to change this world. It takes pragmatism, logic, intelligence, reasoning, facts, proven methods of analysis and implementation. But is that enough? Is it the only way? Many of us tell ourselves it is. Yet in the end when we have accomplished our goal, is it worth it if there is no one around to share it with? Is it worth it if we lose ourselves and the ones we love in the process? For what matters most to people? Money? Power? Five seconds of fame? The praise from the masses, the perceived love and worship from the crowd? More money, power, goods, and resources than we know what to do with? Lavish, extravagant, flamboyant materialistic possession that will one day fade? The pursuit of luxury that cannot define its own value and stay true to its own form? For some, the need is for wealth; for others, power. Others, sex. And still others, love and appreciation. For every person, there is a different need and desire. What is something we can all agree upon that we each need-not want, but need? Do we take the time to truthfully understand what it is? But is there something more? Something that speaks to each person's core. Something that is true in its fruits, yet bitter in the journey taken to understand it? Can it be perceived and understood by the five senses? Is it something psychological, something that the mind needs, but that is blocked by the sensory input taken in from being conscious (and subconscious)? Or is it something of the heart, of the spiritual nature? Is it something that speaks to our core, the unique yet endless depth each person must come to know for themselves by way of their own spiritual journey? What is it that each person yearns for, seeks for themselves? Is it a constant need for all, but understood by only a few? Is it a need that is simple yet is attached to hard to extravagant expectations we put on it? What is it?

As I write this book, part of me does not know why. All I know is that when I investigate this world, I see that people have become consumed by their own creations. In our celebrative state, we lose sight of the liberties that were fought for us, the many advancements that have led to our progress as human beings. As we savor the fruits of the battle, we forget what those who came before us sacrificed. We forget what was fought for. Even now, we think we have won, but the work, the fight, is never done. In the new age, consumerism has consumed us all. We feel the need to consume material possessions because we feel they are the keys to our souls, that can fill the void that rests within us. In this book, I share my thoughts and opinions as to what all people need. For me, what we need is not physical. For the physical will change, wither, and fade, as we do. Yet it is only natural that human beings cling to the things they can hold, they can create, because it is something they can call their own. They can mold it, craft it, so that it reflects themselves in ways that only they know, because we are after all, physical beings on an earthly plane. But I have come to realize that what humans need is never material, but spiritual in nature. I believe everyone has a soul with its own essence and is given a physical form by a creator. I believe that even though we are creatures of flesh, governed by our instincts and impulses, we can be better. I believe that even though we may never know every metaphysical/philosophical truth, we can learn more about ourselves if we are willing to take the journey of self-discovery. I write this book with the realization that I do not definitively know what the world needs or what people need. I am but a human being, a spirit given a physical form like the rest of the souls I walk among. Yet in my heart, I believe that humanity has always avoided the one thing it does not know how to collectively understand … The Human Soul. I write believing that the words I put down, the things I say about the topics I write about are more important than any commodity that has capitalistic value. I write this book because I believe life is more important than the capitalistic lens we use to perceive it. I believe that there is more to people than trying to sell themselves as capital just to make a living. What I write about, I feel, is more significant because it is something we need, but do not know how to discuss. I hope and pray that whoever reads this book will take the time to reflect on its words and content so that they may become a better person. I hope and pray that the souls willing to take the journey of self-discovery will find this book helpful. I hope and pray that the reader will come to appreciate life and its various gifts as I believe all people should. It is my understanding that we all fail to know who we are because we don't know how to start such a journey. We do not know the steps, the procedure, or what to do in certain situations because we are creatures of habit who expect that all that we do in our lives should follow an orderly, logical process. Yet when it comes to the human soul, such a journey is the hardest because such a journey is not orderly, logical, nor a universal process that all people can replicate for themselves. As I write this book, I do not know what to expect or what others will take from it. It is my wish that whether someone reads one page or finishes all the way, they will becomes a better person (in mind, body, and spirit).

LOVE

There is a place in our hearts that knows only darkness. There is a place in our hearts that can only accept the hate, the pain, the fury, the vengeance, the loneliness, and the bitterness given to it. There is a place in our hearts that thrives on negativity. It clings to us; it yearns for us to accept it. For its appeal is easy, its results instantaneous, but what it has in store for us will destroy us. Negativity preys on us when we are weak, when we are beaten, when we are let down. It presents itself when we are at our most vulnerable, when we are confused, yet frustrated. It presents itself to us as a source of strength that will eradicate all that pose a threat to us. When we have known such negativity for so long, it is the only course of action we are aware of and the only thing that we believe makes us feel alive. When we experience it, it brings forth all that we have locked away, all the malice and evil we have suppressed for the sake of appearing good on the surface. Negativity can twist our own perceptions in an instant, turning friend into foe and foe into friend. It reasons with us to make it seem as if the light is the dark, and the dark is the light. Once we accept it into our hearts, we become corrupted by it. It takes all that is good within us, all that is decent in us, all that is moral in us, all that is of a positive nature within us and destroys it.

Such negativity knows only hate. Such negativity knows only pain. Such negativity knows only anger. Such negativity knows only rage. Such negativity knows only how to destroy, how to kill, how to wound, how to hurt. All it knows is of a ravish nature, a brutish nature. When we allow negativity into our hearts, it obliterates all of our virtue. Thus, it will seek to destroy all that is around us. Like a storm, it will consume all in its path. It will devour all that lies in its direction. It will take in all that is kind, gentle, pure, innocent, and of a caring nature and leave behind nothing but chaos. The more we embrace it, the more it consumes us. The more we feed into it, the more it saps from us all that made us good. Like a wildfire, one ember from it can spark the fiercest of flames. Negativity can touch the hearts and minds of those far and wide. It can unite people in ways that good never could. It can move the masses in ways unthinkable to the logical individual. It can make people do things, commit atrocities, they never knew they were capable of. It can bring out the savage within them, the brute within them, the feral beast within them. It can take away all logic, all reason, and any shade of morality a person thought they possessed. Like any drug that does damage to the body, it feels good at first. It creates a state of euphoria, it makes us feel as if we have reached the absolute heights of human pleasure.

At first, we do not notice the toll negativity will exact from us, but by the time we realize it, we are too late. We have become addicted to it. We have become reliant on it, dependent on it. While we thought it would help us, in the end, it only made us lower our guard and be the agent of our own demise, forever a slave to something that has penetrated deeper than what the body could ever feel. By the time we are ready to mount an attack to overcome such a plague, we realize that it is too deep. Negativity connects with us in a way that we cannot live without. Its penetrates to a level that is linked to all that we do. Its merged into a realm of our being that is the epicenter around all that we find meaning. For darkness knows the consumption of light. Darkness knows the absence of truth. Yet the opposite of darkness is light. The opposite of negativity is positivity. And the opposite of hate, is love.

Love, the center of the human emotional spectrum. Of all the sensations in this spectrum, love is the most powerful. When one thinks of love, they think of affection. When one thinks of love, they think of a soul mate. When one thinks of love, they think of a connection that runs deeper than the eye can perceive, what logic can comprehend, and what the human intellect is able to quantify. Love is pure and kind. Love is gentle and sweet in its touch. Love is so simple and yet so powerful. Love is something that is simple, yet complex in nature. For the power love holds is that it is the driving force behind all that we do. It is love that gives way to passion and passion that gives way to commitment. And it is the commitment to what we believe in that affirms or reaffirms our beliefs by way of action. It is love that is the driving force of all we do. It is in love that passion is found. It is in love where intimacy resides. It is in love where the most powerful bonds are forged. What makes love so special is that love cannot be perceived as materialistic things can be perceived, yet we know it is there. Love cannot be seen, heard, touched, smelled, or tasted, yet we know that love is the guiding hand that can wipe away every tear, hear every cry, be the comfort we need when in pain, and be the source of our strength to guide us in our darkest hour. At its core, love is simple. It is not found in extravagant wants or desires. It does not need a high level of social prestige to be accepted by the individual.

At its core, love is found within the heart. It is not found in dollar bills. It is not found in fancy jewelry. It is not embodied, epitomized in the form of sex. It is found within the heart. It is found within the hearts of those who share it intimately. Love can be found in the king of kings as well as the lowest of peasants. Love can be found within the mad man as well as the rational man. Love can be found within the sinner as well as the saint. Love can be found between those who have so little and those who are known to have all that is attainable by the decrees of the world. Yet no matter where love can be found, its true strength comes from the understanding of those who share it. True love comes from the acceptance and the understanding of the two who share it. It comes from the acceptance of their faults, their flaws, their short-comings, the insecurities of their partner, and the growth that comes out of it. Such a perspective does not come from the crowd, the standards of others, or the opinions of society. It does not come from the masses or, the ideas of the times, but from the longing of one's hearts. Love can only be attained by a person when they understand in their heart what it is they call love.

Love may have one definitive meaning, yet at its core, it has an endless depth. Love cannot be quantified, calculated, or measured by the degrees of human intelligence. Love has no limit; there is no limit to what an individual will do in the name of love. There is no boundary, no line a person will not cross to protect/defend/cherish whom they love. Love is something one does not know but feels. It is something you cannot tie to a specific date or point in time, but a feeling that grows more and more as one chooses to embrace it. It is something that you can feel when you have it. It comes from a deep place, a special place, an intimate place, a childlike place in our hearts. As paradoxical as love is, it is something we all need yet deny ourselves. Therefore, a question that all people must ask themselves (but never get the chance) is this: What does love mean to me?

Love is what makes a man lower his masculine guard, and love is what allows a woman to express her femininity. Love is what can bring together two people from different walks of life and allow them to understand each other in ways that would imply they knew each other their whole lives. Love is what can give two people the courage to do what others would consider impossible and make a way when there is no way. Love is what makes a house a home. Love is what makes a meal at the table a memory to be savored for a lifetime. Love is what makes a neighborhood a community. Love is what makes a group of people of the same blood or of different backgrounds a family. Love is what gives sex that much more passion and intimacy. Love is what makes the hardships endured worth going through. Love is what makes going through hell for those we love worth bearing. It is in love that we understand we are human and not machines. It is in love that we cry, we feel, we embrace, we fight, we long for/yearn for something that materialistic possessions could never give us. It is in love that life can be created a-new. It is in love that a moment of pain can be a memory by which an everlasting bond can be forged. It is in love that all we do has meaning. It is in love that one word, one action, one thought can give way to something totally beautiful. It is in love that beauty can take form. It is in love that passion can rise. It is in love that intimacy can be such a binding, powerful, sensual, and unexplainable force housed between those who share it. It is love that makes a king's reign over his people truly justified. It is love that connects people to their leader and a leader to their people. It is love that connects a parent to their children. It is love that makes a husband put his wife before anyone else and forsake all others. It is love that makes a wife love her husband before anyone else and forsake all others. It is love that brings a husband home to his wife every day and night, and it is love that brings a wife home to her husband every day and night. It is love that cooks a meal that can feed a whole family. It is love that is found in each ingredient. It is love that keeps a family together, and it is love that allows the lessons learned from one generation to be passed on to the other. It is love that allows a man or women to accept a child that is not theirs by blood but love them as if they were their own. It is love that gets a parent up early in the morning, to go to work day in and day out so their child can have more than what they could ever have had. It is love that allows us to call something sacred or precious to our hearts and regard it in the way that we do. It is love that can allow a man who has known nothing but negativity his whole life to be easy around the women he loves. It is love that allows a woman who has been hurt by so many to put her trust in a man that she loves and allow him to be the head of the household. It is love that allows a compassionate heart to give back to those who know only selfishness. It is love that makes everything seem possible. It is love that makes a parent stand up to defend their offspring in the face of certain death. It is love that makes us human, that gives us the ability to feel something more than baser instinct and impulsive desire. It is love that makes people more than the machines they create. If we could but search our own hearts, we could see that at some point we can no longer live only for ourselves, but also for others. If we could look within ourselves, could we come to the realization that such an emotion, such a feeling, such a deep and intimate part of our human nature is not a weakness, a hinderance, but a source of our strength? For without love, what are we?

Love, it is so powerful yet always misunderstood. Is love truly sacred? Is love something that speaks to the higher state of being an individual, where they can achieve, if they choose, to be more than their baser instincts? Is love part of the human soul? Does love have to come from a divine place or a divine entity? Was love intended for us mere mortals to have? Were we meant to possess a force so powerful, so rational yet irrational, beyond our comprehension? Were we truly meant to wield such a powerful yet deadly force? As lovely, gentle, sacred, kind, and pure love is, how do we know if the love we seek in our hearts can not only be shared, but understood in the eyes of others? How does a person truly know when they have found the one for them? How can a person know just by looking at another person that they have found true love? Even if we have feelings in the moment for another person, how do we know that such feelings will last forever? How does a person know if their views of love can be embodied the same way by the person they love?

Everyone has wants, desires, dreams, goals, aspirations. Everyone has their own opinions, points of view, ideas, interests, conceptions, perceptions of what something is to them and what it means to them. Many follow the ideas of the era as to what love means. Some people love one another based on what can be obtained, quantified, and calculated. So many see it only in the form of sex. And so many do not know what love is to them. Living by the ways of the world, it is easy to lose oneself to the ideas and perspectives that guide humankind. In trying to fit in and conform to the modern era, we so easily forget what we deeply cherish and neglect our true feelings. So many are romantic and regard love in such an idealistic fashion, but with time, become realistic and pragmatic. So many want a house, a wife, a husband, and a family. But adhering to the norms and philosophy of a society that emphasizes extravagance can cause an individual to see love in the same manner (Over time, this can force them to neglect their view of love for one acceptable to society). So many see life in a lavish manner, yet to them love is simple. They do not desire love to be so over the top that it loses its elegant touch. Yet the demands of their lifestyle and perspective on life are in conflict, causing uncertainty in how they should go about love. They are conflicted by their environment, their desires, their wants vs their needs, their expectations, the expectations of others, and the demands of the current situation, all of which prohibit them from taking the time to ponder what it is love means to them. Love is so misunderstood because it is put into a box. Love is a need of the heart. Love is a longing of the heart. Because love cannot be seen, love cannot be bound. Because love has no end to its depth, there is no image of how it should look or who can find it. Love is not bound by race. Love is not bound by religion. Love is not bound by sex. Love is not bound by color. Love is not bound by region. Love is not bound by socio-economic status. Love is not bound by the traditions of the past. Love is not bound by the ideas of the times. Love cannot be bought, compromised, sold off, nor bargained with. Love is not something that separates two people but brings them together. Love is found in the heart, and because every human being has a heart, every human being is capable of love.

Within the human being is something powerful, something rational, something that no machine can ever feel from its depths because it does not possess it… that is the ability to love. Love is an expression that is too raw to capture, yet it is sophisticated. Love is something that is diametrical, of a dual nature, a contradictory force that is known yet interpreted differently by the light and the dark. Yet love comes from a childlike place in our hearts, an idealistic place that refuses to accept things as they are and to pursue them for what they mean to us.

Love is something that so many deny due to the cold and pragmatic ways of the world. Love is something so many reject and neglect within themselves so as to avoid heartbreak. So many numb themselves to love that they may never feel it. So many have not experienced a love of their own for so long that they may never understand what love is for themselves. So many have come to accept a common consensus of what love is that they may never find it on their own. So many have been tainted by lust that they may never know the difference between the two. No matter how much we deny it, love is something that we all need. Love is something we all long for and desire. While lust is a void that can never be fulfilled, it is love that makes us whole. Yet we settle for lust, for satisfying our base desires. Are we wrong for doing this? Are we wrong to give into the desires of our flesh as they are as much a part of us as the capability to feel love, an emotion that runs deeper than anything we can ever explain? It is the love that we leave behind for our children when we are gone that they remember us for. It is the deeds done in love that people remember us by. It is love that draws others closer to us. It is the deeds done out of love that commands respect. It is love that makes everything we do genuine. It is love that reminds us that we have a heart. No matter who we are, what rank or title we have, what number of resources we have access to, what level of social prestige we may acquire, we all desire love. We all desire that companion who can understand us, know us, see us, love us in a way that only they can. We all want the warmth, the affection, the intimacy, the passion, the attention that only a soulmate can give us. We dream about it from the time we know what it is, we long for it as we get older, and the urge gets stronger the older we get. Yet, we must take the time to understand what love means to us on a basic level, on an individualistic level. We must each search the depths of our own hearts to understand who we are so that we may discover what love means to us. We must learn to let go of what is commonly known or accepted as love and come to our own comprehension of what it is before we compare it to the views of the world. It is only when we have reached our core, our depth, the essence of our soul that we can truly understand our character. And only at that point can we understand what love truly is.

CHAPTER 2

THE HEART
(THE SOUL / THE SPIRIT)

What is it that makes us humans different from the machines and the technology we create? What is it that we human beings hold onto to distinguish us from the various species that surround us? What is it that makes us human? Is it our bodies, our appendages? Is it our minds and our ways of thinking? Or is it our souls, our individual beings, our hearts, which houses our very essence? Has modern man come so far in his technological advancements that he has forgotten that which drives him? Has modern man become so engulfed in science that he has forgotten that it was faith in his works that led to the advancements that he now has? Has modern man relied so much on logic and reason that he has forgotten the principles that helped him along his journey towards a better tomorrow? Throughout history, humanity has always sought improvement. Improvement in ways that could enrich all. Humanity has been driven by the desire to be better than the primitive instincts that governed its ancestors. We looked to religion. We looked to morality. We looked to principles. We looked to science. We looked to technology. We looked to faith. We looked to reason. We looked to logic.

We looked to those who throughout history were examples that led others by the life they chose to lead. Yet no matter how great the sacrifice was, we continue to fall short of the improvement we seek.

So, where does such improvement start? Where does such change occur before it can be understood by all so that it could be adopted by all? Within each of us is something great, something powerful, something that neither science nor any form of analysis will never truly understand. Within us, as human beings, is something that makes us more powerful than our basic instincts, that gives us the ability to look beyond logic and reason and to connect with those around us on a level deeper than the spoken word. What we possess allows us to defy our logical thought process. It allows us to be more than just pragmatic and to see a given situation in a more meaningful context.

Yet we run from it. We run from it because we cannot understand it on a universal level. We run from it because what it means to us is different from what it means to others. We run from it because we cannot explain it the way we want to, and because of that we fear it. We fear it because it cannot be seen, it cannot be heard, it cannot be felt, it cannot be smelled, and it cannot be consumed. We fear it because it cannot be perceived the way we normally perceive the world around us. What makes it so powerful is that it is the driving force of who we are. What makes it so powerful is that it is the core of who we are. It houses the very essence of who we are. It is what separates us from the millions of others. It is the one thing that those who do not know us well can remember us by (even long after we are gone). From it, comes the spirit of humanity. From it comes the strength that lies only in one's heart, not their minds. From such a thing, comes the nature of what we humans deem to be a soul. It is something one is born with, yet few will ever tap into. It cannot be manufactured, created, disassembled, broken down into mechanical parts. It is something intricate, even sophisticated, once an individual takes the time to understand it. Yet at its core, it is raw, full of depth, and the true source of human strength. To be in tune with such a thing is one of the greatest gifts anyone could possess. It is something we humans call the cream of humanity. And while each generation may come to view it differently, they would not be where they are today without it.

Within us is a Heart.

The heart I speak of is not the muscle, but the soul. Within the human heart lies so much. There is to be found so much power, so much potential, so much greatness. Within the human heart is depth. A depth that cannot be calculated, quantified, categorized, or even named. It is that endless depth that makes it hard for us to be understood on a profound level. Such depth cannot be known by the ways of science, but only through self-reflection. Yet we fail to grasp the degree of such depths due to the constraints of human existence. Jobs, occupations, a desire for material possessions make such a journey of self-discovery hard to embark on. I have come to learn that there is no end to the depth of the human soul. There is no limit as to how deep the human heart is. There is no bottom to what we call the human soul.

Within us is a void, an abyss that is foreign because we do not take the time to understand it (We do not know what it means to be our own human being.) We try so vigorously to be who we want others to see us as that we run from who we really are. The more we run, the more we become someone we're not, and we forever run from the depths of our own heart. It is the understanding of our hearts that affects the use of our mind. The use of our mind reflects who we are within. He who is aggressive inward will use all that he has in an aggressive manner. He who is flexible inward will use all that he has in a well-rounded manner. And he who yearns for inward growth will ponder and question more in his mind than he will verbalize out his mouth. It is the mind that succumbs to the spirit, and it is the body that produces the actions of the mind.

What makes the spirit so powerful is that it cannot be contained, captured, measured by the ways of human beings. Yet it is the driving force of person's world allowing them to do what they desires and to see it reflected in the world. So many reject the ways of the heart because theirs is broken. So many reject the heart (their soul) because it cannot be understood by the ways of science. So many cannot understand their heart because so many do not understand one simple truth … we are all different. The heart of one is not the heart of another. That which governs one person is not the same that governs another. We all have free will. We all have freedom of choice to decide what we want to be governed by. It is the initiative of the individual to comprehend that which governs them. It is the initiative of the individual to uncover what drives them, fascinates them, and gives them passion. We all need to understand that which fuels us, drives us, guides us, excites us, frightens us, threatens us, causes us to have doubt, causes us to feel pain, causes us to have love for someone or something. Such realizations cannot be found in the texts of science, in the questions posed by logic, nor in pure analytical inquiry, but by the understanding of our own individuality. Such knowledge of self comes by way of the journey of one's soul. To know thyself is the greatest wisdom anyone can possess. For with it, they can become more than what anyone, even themselves, intended. Such knowledge is imperative. For without it, we will never live a life worth living. Without it, we will merely exist, fading as we walk in the ignorance and arrogance borne of our failure to understanding of our own being.

What is a soul? Just because we cannot physically see it, does it mean that it does not exist? Or is the soul just an illusion created by our mind to explain the individuality of each person? Is it just a concept housed within our psyches, or is there an inner depth to each human being? Is the soul the essence of all human beings? Is it our core, the inner depth that describes us in our entirety? Is it the sum of who we are? Is it our purest form, our most vulnerable form, yet our true form? Is the soul the one thing from which all life emanates? Is it the center of which all things find their meaning, their values, the understanding of their composition? Does it explain why we each have our own set of individual characteristics, our own mindsets, our unique perspectives? Is it that the soul is indeed the true depth, the core, of everyone? Is the soul the reason why we are all different? Does it speak to how those born in different months are said to possess the same unique qualities? Is there a correlation between who we are and how it relates to our individual being? But what lies within our soul? Within our body lies our physical being, a slave to the needs of the flesh.

The mind is a slave to all the stimuli received from the external environment. Each stimulus shapes how one perceives the world. Each feeds into the ego. Each feeds into the development of our conscious mind, and each impacts our subconscious mind. The world around us shapes our thoughts, and it is our thoughts that shape our perception of the world. But what of the soul? What is housed within the soul? Does the soul contain within itself our higher being, or a being that is more refined than that produced by our base human instinct? Do concepts that contradict the logical and reasoning capabilities of the mind bask within the soul? Can faith be found within the soul? Can hope be found within the soul? Can love to found within the soul? Can patience be found within the soul? Can sophistication be found within the soul? Can compassion, kindness, mercy, forgiveness be found within the soul? By understanding one's soul, one's true essence, does one understand themself? Their own internal workings? Their own perceptions, their own characteristics, their own perspectives, the internal world in which they reside? How does one understand the soul? If the soul is something that all people possess, yet the means by which to comprehend it is different for everyone, how do they seek to fathom their inner world and begin such a journey? How does one understand the soul when the soul resides in an external world different from the one in which they live? Thus, how does the external understand the internal, and how does understanding the internal impact the external? Is there truly depth to everyone's character? Is there truly more to us than the eye can see? Is there something that is dormant, mysterious, yet complete within each person that makes up their character? Is that why no two people can ever be the same, regardless of how similar they may be in their beliefs, lifestyle, and views of the world? Is a soul within us? A soul that has allowed humanity through the ages to venture into the unknown, to the point where it surprised itself and become more than what it once was. Was it the inkling of the soul that lead them down that path, or just the inner workings of the mind?

Is there a soul that rests within us?

To neglect the heart is to neglect the soul. To neglect the soul is to neglect that which makes us human. And to neglect what makes us human is to not live at all. We humans are governed by everything. We are governed by life, death, greed, passion, envy, jealousy, wrath, laziness, joy, sorrow, pain, love, kindness, faith, a need to be more than what we currently are, and so much more. An understanding of what drives us is richer than any financial currency. To understand the depths of our own hearts is more fruitful than anything that can bear abundant returns. To understand who we are within will give us a feeling that no amount of money can buy, that no amount of material possessions can give us, that no social status or praise from others can fulfill in our hearts.

It is when we truly understand who we are in ourselves that those outward can no longer affect that which is inward. It is only when we know who we are in our own hearts and know where we each stand within ourselves that we can truly walk down the path that will unfold before us through the years to come. It is in the understanding of our hearts that we understand our own uniqueness, what traits, attributes, and qualities that are more abundant in us than others. It is the uniqueness in us that reflects who we truly are.

To neglect the heart is to neglect the soul. To neglect the soul is to neglect that which makes us human. And to neglect what makes us human is to not live at all. So many reject their uniqueness simply to conform to the times they live in. What society (people) fail to understand is that in uniqueness, true change can form. But for such change to develop, everyone must be given the time and the means to ponder and express their uniqueness. The short coming of every society is the unrealistic desire for all citizens to be the same. But no two Christians are the same. No two artists, philosophers, writers, sculptors, painters, speakers, no two practitioners who study the same art are the same. What is it that makes them different? Their hearts. It is in their heart where their true perspective lies. It is in their hearts where the true meaning of what they learn takes form. It is in their hearts where their ideas form, first being processed in the mind and then enacted through the body.

Some neglect the understanding of their heart due to one thing... principle. To understand the heart is to know one's faults and flaws. To understand one's heart is to know one's short comings. To understand the depths of one's heart is to know their deepest secrets, the harsh truths they have hidden from themselves. To understand one's heart is to see the lies, the faults and flaws, for what they are and not how one desires them to be. Yet can such a person accept such a truth? Can such a person be truthful with what they find? Can such a person take such a harsh yet significant find, such a painful yet truthful understanding, to become a better person? Many do not understand their heart not because they hate principles or lack principles, but because they are unwilling to face such harsh truths and become better because of them.

The Body will always fail you; the Mind will always deceive you, But the Spirit is the true essence of the Individual.

CHAPTER 3

UNITY

What is it about Unity that scares most of us? Why does the coming together of two people or a group of people from different races make us fearful? Is it their cultural differences? The different languages? The difference in perspectives? Religions? The way of life each one believes to be true? Why is it that human beings, having been on this earth for as long as they have, still cannot get past the different shades of pigmentation? Why is it that a person of a different skin tone, can incite fear or a sense of discomfort? Even as Humanity progresses into the technological era, why do we continue old patterns of discrimination? Is there something that separates us, if so, and if so, what is it? Even with science to experiment and explore such differences, what is it within the Human Genome that causes us to have different views on the outside? Black, white, yellow, pink, race, minority, majority, Asian, Hispanics, African, African American, European. There are many different categorizes of groups and subgroups whose roots have become diluted with time. Can we learn to co-exist despite these distinctions, to learn to truly live with each other and not amongst each other? Can we ever get to a point in human history where we as people learn to genuinely respect those who are not like us, who do not look like us, and who are culturally different?

Can we get to a point where we can let go of the stigmas, the stereotypes, the prejudice, the hatred, the racism, the discrimination, the sense that one race is superior to all others? Can we as humanity get to a point where thoughts of treating those unlike us in an inferior manner do not cross our minds? Can a person come to a point in their heart where they see past color, race, ethnic differences? Where they, let a person's character, rather than phenotypical and genotypical differences, be the judge of how they perceive and treat others? For what is the measure of a man? For what is the measure of a women? Is it race? Is it religion? Is it a way of life? Is it the various perspectives? Is it the difference in cultural content? Is it character? Is it works produced? Merit gained through hardship? What is the worth, of a person? At what point can people truly come together? Is the White man smarter than the Black woman? Can a Chinese person offer more insight than a Hispanic individual? Can someone of Arabian descent become better in the eyes of European culture than their ancestors were? Can each of us become more than the mistakes and the shortcomings of our predecessors? Why is it that as modernized and sophisticated as people have become, they still see unity as a taboo? Why do we see the coming together of people of multiple backgrounds the ultimate sin? Why is it that modern society, a society that prides itself on technological sophistication and advancement, critical thinking, and becoming better than its racism and hateful past, refuses to let go of its close-minded nature? Why does it still hold on to its old perspective based on the faults and flaws of its ancestors? Does society contradict itself in what it emphasizes, or is it that a much deeper analysis is needed to determine whether more lies lie beneath the surface?

We all need unity. Unity is the answer to racism. Unity is the answer to closed-mindedness. Unity is the answer to a sheltered perspective. Unity is the answer to the co-existence of human life. It is within unity that true criticism can be found. It is in such criticism that one can truly question their way of life in the eyes of others. It is in unity that ideas and, social constraints can be pondered. The folly of every civilization is found in its inhabitants. The Roman thinks in ways that are good only for Roman society. Hebrews can only see life through the eyes of their own culture. The Greek fail to question the way that only they know. The Mayan will only appease their gods the way the Mayan always has. The Chinese will fight the way only the Chinese know. The dance of the Arabian is that only of the Arabians. The language of Hispanics is only for the Hispanics. The folly is not found in the cultures, the languages, the customs of the group, but in the questioning of such customs through the eyes of the people it benefits. How can one say that they have grown if those who question them only praise them? How can a group of people triumph if they argue with those who mean them no harm? How can an individual say they have reached enlightenment if they do not question and ponder the meaning of their existence? What makes a practitioner of faith say that they have grown in their faith if they only see life from the perspective of the insider and not the outsider? It is in Unity that multiple perspectives can come together to question a topic, an idea, a concept. It is in Unity that stereotypes get put to the test of validity and reliability. It is through unity that social stigmas, and agreed upon views of life can be analyzed from multiple points of view. It is in Unity that a protest has true meaning. It is in Unity that the needs of all can be discussed and addressed. The fault of many societal institutions is a lack of perspective, which is due to a lack of Unity. It is in unity that a person feels appreciated. It is in Unity that a person feels a sense of belonging. It is in Unity that a voice becomes powerful.

Many Institutions are based on a failure to consider the role Unity in their pursuits. They fail to understand that a united community is a stable community. They fail to understand that in unity, economic prosperity takes hold; an example is (the Silk Road). They fail to understand that in unity, crime stops itself. They fail to understand that in Unity, a better tomorrow takes shape and is given form. Unity is what turns a neighborhood into a community. It is what makes a ruler's regime seem blessed rather than tyrannical. Unity is what makes all that we do worthwhile. It is in unity that the deeds of one are appreciated, as they are felt by and affect all those around them. It is in unity that everyone works together so that we may all prosper. It is in unity that one deed is meaningful, especially when combined with the deeds of others (to ensure the prosperity of all). A community cannot live divided, for that is not co-existing. And a community cannot live divided, because all who dwell there will not be living at all, but suffering.

While such an endeavor may not be worthwhile at face value, such a pursuit is the purest of them all. Without unity, people will never grow. They will put their trust in machines or creations of their own making to raise the next generation. But reliance on creations without the essence of what it means to be human will only produce people who do not know their nature, and will only further ignorance and arrogance in the world.

Yet many ask, where is unity found? Can it be found in one's community? Is it found in the strength of numbers? Is it found in the collective consensus? In the diversity of, options to choose from? Or is the important issue that the concept of Unity itself is neglected, misunderstood, and feared because of a lack of understanding. So many do not want to be unified with those around them because they themselves have not questioned their own perspective. Unity is not accepted because (in the eyes of some), there is no money, no profit to be gained from it. So many see opportunities for wealth and success borne of the hatred, despair, and separation of people. Some see profit in war, aggression, disapproval, yet I beg to differ. There can be so much more gained in the coming together of people. For each group of people, each race, each culture brings something that the other does not. Each brings their own uniqueness, their own goods, their own resources, their own ideas, their own opinions, and their own ways of implementing them. We can find so much richness in the unification of people. There is so much to be gained in the coming together of different perspectives and ideas. The true wealth of the people lies not in their material goods, but in unification as a society. So many neglect Unity because they do not understand it, and misinterpret it. But what is unity? What does it mean to be unified? Does unity relate only to a specific group of people? Does it speak to communities? Does it speak to religion or cultural backgrounds? Does it speak to demographics? Living in this world, I have come to realize that there will always be those who can never look past the surface of another person's appearance. There are some who can only live in the bubble they create, and prefer to be closed off in their own version of reality. There are some who are too afraid to question differences because of the fear or rejection that often results from contemplating the social norm. Will we ever know what Unity means absolutely if it cannot be applied to so many aspects of life?

The unity I speak of is of people. How much longer can people live divided? How much longer will it take for people to see beyond skin color, to understand that it is what is inside that counts? How many more wars, abominable acts will it take for people to realize that a sheltered perspective is one that will never last? How much more will it take for all people to try to live with each other and not amongst each other? What makes those of European descent better than those of African descent? What makes the Chinese more sophisticated than Hispanics? What makes any group of people better than the next? Is it intrinsic? Is it their societal contributions to the world? Is it the texts that served as the backbone for the creation of some of man's greatest achievements? Is it the methods, forms, or ways of thinking that spurred technological advancements? Advancements that brought mankind out of the caves and into the seats of the kings and queens, and others who ruled empires and dynasties for centuries? What separates one person of one race from another? What makes one group of people better or less than the next? And where is such a difference found?

I have come to find unity within people. While on the outside we are different, our own histories not so similar, within us beats the same heart, breathes the same breath, and longs for the same thing that every living soul desires, just in a different way. Unity is always found amongst the people, not the things we create.

I have seen it with my own eyes. I have seen the hope of the future, the unity amongst all people. It may not be found in the lavish life of the rich and wealthy, but among the masses. I have seen it in the laughter of conversation, the parties and festivities of those who call each other friend. I have seen it among those who look beyond skin color and have love. I see it in the joy, fun, and innocence of children playing. I see it in the heart-to-heart conversations of the common man. I have come to find unity among those who struggle together. I have come to find unity among the neighbor living in the community. I have come to find unity among those who have little compared to those who have a lot. I have come to find unity among the simple-minded, the common folk. I have come to see that so many misunderstand and are intimidated by the concept of unity because they seeing it as something that must take place on a large scale, fail to see it when it occurs on a small scale. So many see the unification of people all over the world, but not those we live among. So many see unity in the sense of equal treatment, respect, access to goods and resources for all, but what does that mean on a small scale? So many preach unity, but what do they have to show for it? If we human beings are to treat the person next to us with equality, respect, and fairness, how and where does that start? Does unity start with the revision of societal principles, morals, and philosophies that govern the use of goods and resources? Does it start with the revision of the social norms we create, adopt, and enforce? Does it start with how we portray those who are not like us? Does it start with short conversations that are controversial but that involve topics that need to be discussed to overcome certain barriers? While others may not find a reason to fight for unity, it is not a lost cause. Unity is not an idealistic thought that can never be set in motion. It is within all of us to be advocates for a better tomorrow. It is within every man, woman, and child to tear down the social stigmas of previous generations. It is within each person to bridge the gap that those before us would not or were afraid to take. Although people do not always share such an opinion, many want the best for the next generation. But is what is best goods, services, resources, wealth passed down from one generation to another? Or is it the questioning of outmoded traditions by those who rebel against the status quo? In the future, what will the world think of unity? Will people adopt the philosophy of the previous generation, falling into their ways? Or will they look they look at the mistakes of those who preceded them, and seek to be better? Will they question the ideas of the generation coming up, as their parents did about theirs?

While the pursuit of unity is idealistic, it is worth achieving. People may never learn to fully cooperate with each other due to their free will, attitudes about those who are different, and outlooks on life. But co-existence can be achieved if all are willing to come to the table and see each other as equals rather than adhere to the terms of dominance that will continue the destruction of others. While ethnicity, demographics, and place of origin will always be seen from the outside, unity can shine if intellectual integrity and emotional understanding can plow through hate and ignorance to reach a better understanding.

CHAPTER 4

KINDNESS

Of all the things in this world, kindness is the hardest to find. Of all the things in this world, kindness is one of the hardest to adopt. And of all the things in this world, kindness is one of the hardest to appreciate. It is ironic that kindness is something all people cherish but many see as weak or inferior. Many see kindness as something for the peasant to adopt (because they have nothing) while those at the top see kindness as something their enemy uses to their advantage. When I look at the world, I see that many do not understand the simple act of kindness. When I think of kindness, I think of an act done out of appreciation and admiration from one person to another. When I think of kindness, I think of an act done for others who are deserving of it, whether they know it or not. I see kindness as a force that can ease the soul and put the mind to rest. When I see kindness, I think of a fortress of solitude. I see it as a quality that reminds us that there are good people in the world. I see it as a reminder that good can blossom though evil is ever present.

When I think of kindness, I wonder why. Why would one person show such an act to someone they deem fitting when they do not do so for others? Is it out of respect? Admiration? Loyalty? Or a caring for qualities in that person that others do not see? The need for kindness is so great, but we do not know it. Can acts of kindness be the key which opens the door to the release we need? Are they a breath of fresh air that marks a new beginning, one that we so desperately need? Does kindness signify to us the weight we bear on our shoulders? Do the lack of acts of kindness reveal to us the price of the life we chose to lead?

People of the modern era have forgotten what an act of kindness can do. The modern era is so fueled by competition, greed, self-importance, a fast-paced lifestyle, and the desire for money that its inhabitants have forgotten how much one act done with care can do for them. Everything is done for the benefits, the rewards it can yield. Everything is done in a transactional manner, with no personal feelings attached. It is hard to cherish anything because value is seen only in terms of materialistic return, rather than being admired for its intrinsic value. Because many have forgotten small acts of kindness done for them in the past, they also forget what such acts mean. Living in the modern era, such acts are rare, and People have forgotten what kindness is. However, that does not mean kindness is something that has moved on and become one with the wind. That does not mean that kindness is only for the weak and not for the strong. That does not mean that the one who is kind is not inferior to the person next to them. All acts of kindness must come from a genuine place rather than for the advantage one might gain over the next person. In a day and age where things are done for selfish reasons, a true act of kindness can lift up those broken down to the point where they believe they can never rise above that which afflicts them.

But what is kindness? Is it an emotion? Is it a courtesy? Is it a lesson learned through deep appreciation? Is kindness a way of life, a reflection of character, a way to treat people? Is kindness the antidote to pain? Is it a cure for the pain so many have on a level that cannot be seen from the outside? Is kindness the warmth provided to us when we are deserving of something, even when we are not worthy of it? Is it the affections felt from another for reasons we do not know at first? Is kindness something that just any one person decides to bask in? What does choosing to be kind do to a person's character? Does being kind show that a person is weak and complicit? Does being kind show that a person is a push over and avoids conflict? Does kindness dictate that a person is willing to be trampled over and continues to do so because they do not know any other way to treat others? Or is there more to kindness than what others see? Does being kind speak to strength and maturity? Do people who treat others with kindness do so because the other person has given up on such an act? Because the other person may have known only neglect their whole life? Do people who treat others with kindness see that some who are malicious or cruel were once treated in such a manner themselves? Do people who treat others with kindness do so because they see that a lack of kindness will only breed cruelty?

So, what does it say about the character of a person who treats others with kindness when they are treated the opposite? Does it speak to their courage? Does it speak to their strength? Does it speak to the wisdom of the person who employs it? Does it speak to acts of love or hope in other people? Does it speak to a faith that the deeds performed for others will have a positive effect?

How far can an act done out of kindness go? Can it be seen by those who watch others employ it? Can it be seen a bystander? Can true acts of kindness (those done from the heart) reach the inner depths of the human soul? Can they penetrate the strongest and thickest of hides and soften the hardest and, coldest of hearts? Can true acts of kindness heal the wounds resulting from the deepest of pain, the pain that the naked eye cannot see? Can kindness give people hope that somewhere in this world there is a better way to bring together, those of all walks of life, to exist amongst each other? And can it give people faith that such simple acts, seen or unseen, can echo across time and have an impact on those we touch and those we've touched but never seen? Can acts of kindness touch the lives of those we will never meet? Touch the depths of their hearts in a way that can help them give others the comfort, the support, and the warmth all humans need? Can kindness be a fortress, a wall which shields us, protects us from the darkest corners of our hearts? Can it be the line in the sand, the boundary drawn that reminds us what it is we fight for? Can kindness be the thing in our heart that reminds us of what we can be if we let the pain, the hurt, the anger, the rage, the embarrassment, the shame, the guilt go? Can kindness allow us to see the good that lies within our own heart as well as the hearts of others (even if they cannot see it themselves)? And can kindness remind us that at the end of the day, it is something we all need?

Why is kindness so hard to find? What is it about kindness that makes it so rare but, so potent, so powerful, soothing, warming and gentle? Is it a defense mechanism to reject most of the people we come into contact with that makes kindness so hard to find? Is it that we are not trusting by nature? Is it that to survive in this world, we develop defenses according to the environment we are raised and live in? And as we venture into the unknown world, we strengthen our hide as we are not as protected by our parents or loved ones as we once were? But in doing so, what do we give up? Do we give up our morals to survive? Do we give up our Idealistic ways of thinking to survive? Do we give up the dreams or the hopes of a better world we once had as a child? In doing so, do we lose the one thing we need most to survive in this world…our soul? Or is it that kindness is misunderstood as a whole? If kindness is limited to the scope of the understanding of the person who adopts it, what then is its meaning? Is kindness meant to have one meaning? If it is, does that suggest that individual acts of kindness should occur in a specific manner? But if kindness has no true form in how it is used, does that mean it has more than one meaning? How does one come to find its true meaning (if there is one)? Is the reason why so many misunderstand kindness because they have never experienced it? Is it that some people have only known shame, neglect, rejection, silence, loneliness? Is it that some people have only known pity, hatred, torment, abuse, violence, anger, cruelty, and malice? Is the reason why so many do not know kindness because they are so far gone? Have they gone over the edge, given into the dark abyss in their heart to such an extent that they cannot come back? Is it that they lack the will or the strength to fight such an internal battle? Is it that some people have tried repeatedly, but every time they did, it got worse? Is it that everyone does not have a strong will, a strong support system, a strong mind, or enough faith to get going? Is it that some people tried to tell others, but it fell on deaf ears? Is it that some people tried to speak about it, but they did not know how? Or is it that some people once believed in such a thing? They believed in kindness and treating other with kindness. But those they loved the most, cherished the most, looked up to the most taught them to shun kindness? Is it that others once shared the same dream, but were told differently, treated differently? They were spurned, beaten, laughed at, made fun of, treated as weak or inferior? Is it that some tried, but the more they did, the more the anger built up? Is the reason why kindness is misunderstood because being kind is not within our primal human nature? Is it that kindness is something that a person must look deep into their heart to find? Is it that to be kind is to take a journey of the soul? And is that the reason why kindness is misunderstood, because we each must venture into our soul to understand what that is to each of us and we do not?

What does it take for a person to accept a kind act from another? Will kindness be something that society and the world will ever understand? Or is kindness something that everyone will come to understand the same way? Is kindness something meant to be understood by the masses? Is kindness something that we as human beings are capable of even if we do not know it? Is kindness something that can be taught, like most subjects, in school? What does it take for a person to see the good in others if others see their kind acts as a sign of weakness or as a sign of acceptance?

So, what does it take for kindness to be seen and understood by others? Does it take faith? Does it take commitment? Does it take strength? Does it take loyalty? Does it take trust? Or does it take the realization that to see the change you want in this world, it starts with you? Is that where kindness is found, is it found in the heart? Does it start with the individual? Does it start with the feeling of putting good in the world? Does it matter who wields it? Can the acts of kindness done by the peasant go on to have more meaning than those done by the rich and powerful? Is one act of kindness greater than another if it is done from the depths of one's heart? If kindness is to grow and blossom in the world, what will it take to encourage it? Will it take each person understanding that every day is a blessing? Will it take each person appreciating all the things we have but take for granted? Will it take society to stop worshipping things that hold decaying value? Will it take people understanding what it is we truly can have amongst ourselves? Will it take family, friends, loved ones, significant others to remind us that kindness can exist in this world? For kindness to be present in the world, does it take action that goes against what the world tells us and what people believe? Will it take people coming together by understanding their differences? Will it take each person being able to see the worth of a person by their actions and not their appearance? Will it take the unification of the masses to break down the barriers of hate, cruelty, malice to let kindness bloom? Should we each search our own soul to reach such an understanding? Should we each learn to forgive the acts of the past? Should we each learn to find our triggers, our wounds, and let them go? Should we come clean about what is on our hearts, let the pain go, and live a life not chained to the things that restrict us from being the better person we all can be? Should we change the ways of the world? Should we change the old systems and make one founded on the moral principles that will allow us to strive towards the better people we can be? Is such a thing possible or even attainable? Is such a thing realistic and practical in its meaning? And if it is possible, is it something that we are all deserving of?

What will it take for others to appreciate kindness?

What will it take to see all people be treated with kindness?

What will it take to see kindness blossom in this world?

COMPASSION

Compassion, a simple word with a profound meaning. When I think of compassion, I see kindness fused with forgiveness. When I think of compassion, I think of someone performing an act out of kindness for a person who needs it the most. When I think of compassion, I see it as the encouragement that is given to another, that reminds them that they are not alone. Compassion is the feeling we get when we realize that we are not alone in our suffering. It is the brotherly love found among men, and the sisterly love embraced among women. Compassion is the sympathy we feel when we confide in someone who understands our plight. Compassion is the tenderness, the gentleness we feel when we meet someone who understands our pain when those around us do not. Compassion is the heart's way of letting us know that we are not alone in our suffering. Compassion is the feeling we get when others are concerned about our suffering. Compassion is being concerned about the misfortunes of others. It is a compassionate heart that heeds the call of the sick. It is a compassionate heart that heeds the call of the lonely, the mistreated, the abused, and the poor. It is the compassionate person who can change the world.

Yet so many lack compassion from those different from them. Many see compassion in a one-sided manner. Some see it as concern for those who look like them and identify with them. Some view compassion as only a physical action, a superficial attempt to show others that they care, when deep down they do not. Others see compassion as acknowledging a person's pain or misfortune without offering concrete assistance. Yet deep down compassion is so much more. It is what allows change to be brought about in the world. Compassion is the driving force of those who seek to better the world for the sake of mankind. It is a compassionate person who recognizes the needs of all people and works to see that others prosper as they do. It is a compassionate person who looks past themselves and what they have achieved to better those around them. It is a compassionate heart that warms those who are in dire need. It is a compassionate heart that understands the struggles of those who have not voiced their concerns. It is a compassionate heart who sees that the suffering of one is the suffering of all. To have compassion is a rarity; the ways of the world and basic human nature make it difficult. Many see compassion as a weakness shared amongst peasants; others, as something in short supply that people need. To have compassion is to have strength of character. To have compassion is to know that one person's struggles may not be the same as another's, yet we all struggle and need encouragement.

To have compassion is to live with the knowledge that not all hope and faith in humanity is lost. It takes those who were once lonely and broken-hearted to lift up those who are low and feeling discouraged. It takes those who are strong enough to pick themselves up and become better than what they once were to offer the helping hand people need when others cast them to the winds. Compassion is something possessed by those who have not given up on others, and who are willing to help someone become that which they always could be (whether they knew it or not). Many lack compassion because they suffer from the worst thing of all… a broken heart. A broken heart lacks so many things, and compassion is one of them. A broken heart lacks all the positive components: peace, love, faith, hope, joy. At the same time, it accepts all the negative components: anger, rage, hatred, malice, pain, loneliness, all of which lead to suffering. It is a broken heart that cannot accept compassion, (for negativity cannot accept positivity). Such a heart not only rejects compassion, but fears it because of the weakness it may signal to others. A broken heart fears compassion because it does not understand it. It does not understand how something so pure, so good, so genuine can exist in this world, and can be resilient and prosper after being beaten down time after time. And what a broken heart does not understand, cannot comprehend, it will seek to corrupt.

Many lack compassion because they do not suffer, or do not experience the same kind of suffering others do. Yet suffering is suffering. The downfall of most people is that they compare their suffering to that of others. Such a thing does speak to the different circumstances and factors that governs one's way of life. But is it the struggle that matters or the triumph brought about by overcoming the struggles? Many lack compassion because compassion was not given to them. Many lack compassion because they do not know what compassion is. Many lack compassion because of the ways of the world. To survive in an unknown environment, it is logical to neglect the needs of others to meet your own. A survival instinct is necessary to thrive in such an environment and, turning that instinct off is hard. The world can be cold, brutal, unrelenting, and unforgiving. To cope, we exchange the idealistic thinking of our childhood, our imagination, with a pragmatic perspective in order to survive. In doing so, we become more aware of our present reality, but give up on the hope and faith that things can get better. Many lack compassion because of their perceived weakness, a weakness they think others will take advantage of. It is that weakness they think will make them a target for mistreatment and manipulation. But is that true? Is compassion for those who suffer in a way that makes living harder for them than it is for others? Is compassion only for those who cannot help themselves no matter what they do and how hard they try? Does a man who can see need more compassion than a blind man? Does the rich man need compassion when compared to the poor man?

In other words, should compassion be given to someone based on their needs, struggles and current situation?

Should we be compassionate to others because we pity them or because they are truly deserving?

Should a person be compassionate because it is seen as the right thing to do, or because it is the only way that the soul can truly be healed?

But what is compassion? Is compassion an emotion, an emotion we feel when others help us in a way that we cannot help ourselves? Is compassion the warmth we get when we realize we are not alone in our struggles? Is compassion the benevolence of the heart? Is it the gem of humanity? Is compassion the acts of genuine concern that can heal the heart, ease the mind, and calm the body? Is compassion a reminder that no matter how strong, how weak, how rich, how poor, tough, or how resilient one may be, we all need someone to help us? Is compassion a reminder that no man, no women, no child can achieve all things alone? Is compassion a reminder that no matter how much we may achieve through merit, we will forever have struggles that we cannot get through alone?

The standard definition of compassion is pity or sympathetic concern for the sufferings or misfortunes of others. When you look at the masses, at the different societies that make up the world, compassion is always dependent on the person who understands it. So, is compassion based on the perception and understanding of the person who comprehends it? All people want others to adopt a compassionate outlook that benefits themselves and those around them. But is such a thing possible? So, should compassion have a standard definition if all people perceive it differently? Should one act of kindness be held to a higher standard than others? If one person donates five dollars or five loaves of bread, and one person donates ten dollars or ten loaves of bread, which act should be held in higher esteem? Should the one with greater quantity, or the one with higher quality, be held in a higher regard? Or should people learn to see that it is not the parts, but the sum of the work done that matters most? Are the compassionate acts of the king held in higher regard than those of the commoner? Do the compassionate acts of the commoner have more meaning to others than those of the peasant? In other words, does compassion have more meaning depending on the person who embodies it? Who is to say which act has the most value? Is it judged by the mouths fed? The hearts warmed? The bodies clothed? The smiles put on another's face? Is it by the lives impacted? Are the seeds of compassion found in money used to meet the needs of the people? Is compassion found in the resources gained and allocated? Is it found in the power one wields over others? In the decisions that will have the greatest effect on the lives of those it impacts? Or is it found in the understanding of the person who comprehends it? So, will compassion mean the same to everyone and will everyone express it in the same way? Is there an ideal way to show compassion? If so, is that a good thing or a bad thing? And in what ways should we express compassion?

Most people say they need more compassion in their lives. Some try to find it amongst others. Some try to find it through acts of philanthropy, community involvement, or by giving to others what others never gave to them. Yet despite their best efforts, some people, try but can never find compassion in the ways they seek. So where is compassion found? Is it found in one region or another? Is it Indigenous to one group of people? Is compassion something given to us from a higher power? Is it found in the acts of kindness done for others? Is it found in the dollars given to the poor, the food given to the hungry which fills their bellies, the clothes given to the naked bodies that provides warmth, the knowledge passed on to the next generation so they may use it in ways their predecessors never thought possible? Is compassion found through hardship? Is it found by the trials of life and the experiences we endure each day? Is it found in the experiences, or in the lessons learned from them, that make us a better person (if we choose to be)? Is compassion something we are all born with? Is it part of our human psyche? Is it something embedded in our soul? Is compassion something that all people are capable of? Is it found within a certain type of person? Can the murderer have compassion just as the innocent can? Can the sinner have compassion just as the saint can? Can the king, who wields so much power, have the same compassion as the peasant, who has nothing to call their own? Is compassion dependent on which part of the social ladder one occupies? Can the rich, with all their wealth, power, influence, and prestige, have compassion while being so detached from the people their decisions impact on a day-to-day basis? Can those at the very bottom, those lower than the commoner, have compassion for others in a way that the rich and common folk cannot? Does the level of compassion one has for others depend on how much they make, their professional occupation, the amounts of wealth they have gathered over the course of their existence? Is compassion based on where one was born, how one was raised, one's level of education, what one inherits, or is it something more?

What makes the person who has compassion different from others? Is it that such a person took a journey inward to understand what it means to them, and in doing have a deeper level of understanding? So, is compassion found within the heart? Does it start within the heart? Is it found in the daily labors done by everyone? Is it determined by social status, wealth gained, resources acquired? Does one group have a deeper understanding of compassion than another? Thus, is compassion borne of environmental circumstances, the challenges one will face throughout their life, or by the content of each person's own character?

I am of the belief that, like all things, it starts out small (every act counts) before it can become big. I'm not one to judge whether one act of compassion is greater than another and one worthy of a higher praise than the other. But I do believe that the greater the act, the more it speaks to the true character of that individuals soul and the lengths they are willing to go to carry out the endeavor.

So why do we as people need compassion? We need it because no man, women, or child is strongest alone. Each of us has our strengths as well as our weaknesses. What we lack, others make up for. It is those with compassion that bring goodness to the world and warmth to the hearts of others. It is compassion, as well as kindness and other attributes, that makes a leader loved, a hero praised by those they save, and someone a role model to others. What makes them matter is that they understand the struggles of others and sympathize with those who look up to them. But it is the acts they do that matter. For no amount of money, fame, power, prestige, or pity can give a person compassion, to go on to change the world for the greater good.

It is compassion that can heal the wounds of the past and correct the wrongs of the generations that came before us. It is compassion that allows a king to not rule his people, to not govern his people, but to love his people. The gem of compassion is at work when a leader fights for those who cannot fight for themselves, when a stranger can identify with the poor and be a Good Samaritan in their eyes. To fight for what is worth fighting for, it is compassion one must have. Compassion is what allows a person to understand how the deeds of one cannot hinder the lives of all it will impact. It is compassion that allows a person with a broken heart to heal. It is the acts done out of compassion that can wipe away the tears of the abused, the helpless, the defenseless. It is compassion that brings all people together so they may change the world in ways their ancestors never could. It is the compassionate individual who will never give up, who will fight to the very end, so that every need is met and every oppressed voice is heard. It is a compassionate heart that hears the cries of the mute and becomes their advocate. It is a compassionate ruler that can make the throne a symbol that only the purest of hearts will step up to and lead their people justly. It is the dreams, aspirations, and imaginations of a child coupled with the intelligence, wisdom, and understanding of an adult that can change the ways of the world for eons to come. Compassion stops the powerful from controlling the hearts and minds of all who bow before them and from corrupting their soul. It allows us to understand what we each fight for by reminding us where we come from, (the struggles faced and endured that culminate in the better person we are today). It is compassion that allows us to love others, and treat them as they should be treated because it is compassion that allows us to sympathize with them. It is compassion that connects us to others. It is that bond forged from struggle that allows others to venture to places where others would not dream of and do what those before us deemed impossible. It is compassion that gives character meaning. For it is a compassionate heart that is not only the greatest gift to the world but that brings the greatest gifts to the world.

Why do people need compassion? It is simple … we all suffer in some way from a broken heart. And no matter how much we come to possess materially there is nothing like the warmth we feel in our hearts when surrounded by others who love us, the warmth that comes from a place that could only come about by way of a compassionate heart.

CHAPTER 6

TRUST

cannot recall a true bond shared that was not founded in trust. I cannot fathom a friendship not built on the foundations of the principle of trust. To think that trust is but a word used to describe the degree to which one person finds comfort in another person, with whom they can share their most intimate fantasies and sacred secrets. To think that such a person would use the principle of trust to decide to what degree to distinguish one individual from another. Trust appears to be a simple word. Yet when taken to its core, its meaning, its depth, and at its highest heights, it is a word by which all people live. Trust is at the core of all friendships, the principle by which all ties (mundane or intimate) are bound. Trust is what allows two kings to rule their respective lands without entering a war. Trust is what allows a parent to trust their child to become the person they raised them to be. Trust is what allows two people to be intimate and love one another in a way that only those two can. Trust is what all organisms strive for to survive. The wolf pack trusts that the alpha will not lead them astray. The pride has trust that the lion in charge will not lead them to their demise. The inhabitants of an empire put their trust in their elected/appointed leader to lead them, not rule them. In all things, it is trust that we all seek. To trust is not to rule. To trust is not to oppress. To trust is not to dominate. To trust is to have faith. Faith in that the one you trust will not lead you astray. Faith that the one you put your trust in will not abuse it. Faith that your trust will be reciprocated. What makes trust so sought by all is that a bond grounded in trust is a bond forged in true friendship. Trust cannot be bought, sold, or supplied, but it is coveted. Trust must be earned. While fools look to buy what can only be gained by principle, the wise understand that what is sought by all does not have a price. And so it is the same with trust. Trust comes by experience, it comes by faith, it comes with time. It is not grasped through manipulation, power, politics, money, witty remarks, or elaborate schemes. It comes by way of commitment, character, honesty, faith, and originality. To trust is to believe. To believe in others, yourself, or in something that you deem greater than you will come to you in a way that you need it most. To trust is not to look at what you have, but what can be. Trust is a longing that the heart desires. It is an ingredient that all life forms require to survive. Trust is what allows human beings to be more than mere instinct and impulse. Trust is what gives every action taken that much more meaning, and it goes deeper than what the eyes can see.

Trust is a very tricky topic. It is the one thing that can make friendships last a lifetime, or it could be the very thing that kills people in the end. Trust is never easy because, like faith, is something that can't be found in data, statistics, schematics, or by any other logical/analytical means. It is something that comes from the heart and is founded on the belief that what is shown/given to one human being or a group of people will be reflected/reciprocated by those who initiated it in good faith.

For what is trust but a word given a meaning? What is trust? A longing of the heart? An inkling of our essence, our desire to connect with others in a way that is genuine and pure? Is trust merely a concept? Is it a concept used to describe what we as humans see as the coming together of all things on one accord? Is trust the one idea that allows all organisms to come forth and exist in harmony? Is it then a key component of harmony, tranquility, and unison? Is trust the underlying principle that keeps the universe, the various ecosystems working together in a way us mere mortals cannot comprehend? Is it a language that is unspoken, yet understood by all races and species? Is it more than just the foundation by which all bonds are formed and should be formed? Is trust simply a component? Is it just an idea, used to engender respect for another? Does the meaning of trust depend on a person's understanding or interpretation of it? Or can trust be something more? If taken to its highest heights, can trust be the principle that ends all wars? Can trust be the principle by which all people can live together in harmony, despite their differences? Can trust be the degree to which all people are judged? Can it be the leap of faith to venture into the world of tomorrow in a realm of endless, unforeseen, and frightening possibilities? Can trust be the true building block by which people understand one another? Is it contextual, systematic, circumstantial? Is trust a response fueled by our survival instincts to adapt to the demands of our immediate environment? Is trust built upon the fleeting things in the world by which all people distinguish themselves? Is trust based on who has the better goods or more resources? Is trust built on someone's state in life, like recognition and who is more well-known?

But what does it mean to trust? To put that which you treasure most into the hands of others, or something greater than yourself. To have faith in others or in something that is greater than what you know. Is it wise to put your trust in something abstract, even if it can yield concrete results? Is it wise to put your trust in something that is only physical? Is it wise to conform to popular opinion, to put your trust in something that everyone else sees as trustworthy or profitable? Is it wise to put our trust in those we do not know? Or should we put our trust in only those known to us? When a person puts their trust in someone or something, either (physical or abstract), how do they evaluate the outcome? Is it by the faith gained? The rewards and benefits gained? The knowledge gained? The wealth or resources gained? Is it that we judge how a bad situation turned out for the better good? Is it that we judged the trust we put in others by what they choose to do with it? If they became better for it, can we say that our trust worked out for the greater good in the end? If they became worse, can we say that we should have let logic and reasoning been our guide? In a slightly different context, if we put our trust in a situation we know is bad and it turns out to be good, can we say that we were right to have faith in what we believe? If so, should we continue to do so in all situations? And conversely, if we put our trust into a bad situation that turns out to be worse, were we wrong to use trust as a means of judgement rather than logic and reasoning? So by what means do we determine how, what, when, where, and who to trust?

Where is trust found? Is it found on the battlefield? Is it found in the bedroom? In the emotional trenches? In the heart? Is it found among friends? Is it found among strangers? Is trust something only a married couple can have? Is it something we can have in people we consider long-term friends? Can trust be found in the darkest of places? If two people are intimate and share a lovely moment, is there trust in that moment? Can trust be found in a society that has not experienced it? Can trust be found in an ecosystem that does not behave in a way that humans understand? Can the peasant find a sense of trust in those in the same predicament? Can the king find trust in those within his court? Can the queen find trust in her subjects knowing she is a woman in a man's world? Can a child trust their parents to lead them down the right path? Can the critical thinker trust in their ability to use logic and judgment even when they are biased? Can the philosopher trust that their speculations about the abstract and the unknown are correct? Can the mathematician trust in the equations set forth to explain the deeper mysteries, those that exceed comprehension?

All people put their trust in what they do know and shun what they do not. All people believe they know in which direction to go, yet few will ever be certain. What is trust if we do not know where it can be found? If trust was found in only one place, could we say that such a source is genuine? Or would we think that source was corrupted, and question whether trust even exists? Is it then a good thing that trust does not have a definitive shape or construct for everyone, but that each person comes to find in the way they know how? Is it a shame that trust does not have a universal standard that all people can come to accept? If trust is a concept that has one meaning, and a person does not understand that meaning, can we say that they do not know what trust is, nor that they have it? What if that person is familiar, has the characteristics of what we deem to be trust, and shares their ideas with others? Do groups of people understand only a concept of trust that is specific to them? And if they do not hold the common consensus on what trust is, can those on the outside be critical of such a group? Is trust then found within the contexts of the moment? Is trust found within the character of the person who professes it? Is trust then found within the mind of the one who wields it? Is trust something innate? Is it in the emotional spectrum? Human consciousness? The depths of the human heart? Is trust spiritual, found in the divine, in a realm that is felt but not seen?

In my opinion, the most difficult part of defining trust is that we may never know its origins in the sense that we may never know why we adopt it when all else fails us. The sources of trust are fragile and easily threatened by inner turmoil, the scrutiny of others, and the ways of the outside world. Such sources are the ego, pride, the mind, the spirit, human nature, emotions, values, beliefs, our very existence.

Is trust something that we are deserving of? If not, then what will take its place? And if it is something we deserve, why do we need it? From an evolutionary point of view, we are nothing but instincts and impulses trying to meet the demands of the environment we live in. So, why do we need trust? Why do we feel the need to put our trust in things both large and small? Why do we put our trust in things that are both real and abstract? Why do we need to trust ourselves? Why do we need to trust others?

I have come to find that it is trust that engenders the most comfort in human beings. Trust is what eases the tension between people and allows them to open up. And it is trust that allows a person to… trust others as well. I have come to find that trust is the one thing that each person must work for. Trust is the one thing that any person, no matter the social status, can have for themselves and can use to dictate those within their inner circle. So, to some extent, trust allows for a degree of control. It is a simple construct, available to all. I have come to find that all people need trust because at the end of the day, it is all we have. Impulses and instinct will get a person far, but trust can give a person the courage to take leaps and bounds. Trust is the one thing that can stop tribes from killing each other and allow them to live in harmony. And trust is the one reason why people are willing to try to understand one another. Whether in ourselves, an object, other people, or in a force greater than our own, trust is the one thing that allows us to put aside past differences and enjoy peaceful existence. Yet why trust the stranger, the uncommon Individual, the anomaly, the rarity, the unprecedented, that which is not accepted by all, the unknown? Why trust what we do not know, what we do not understand? Why should such things be deserving or worthy of our trust? How can we trust them when we do not know what they will yield? Why trust them if they offer no consistency? Why put our trust in what is yet to come? Why should one be worthy of our trust and not the other? Can we be trusted with the knowledge that we possess? Can we trust our own judgment of what we know? Can we be trusted with the faith others have in us when they are emotionally vulnerable? Can we have faith that when we ourselves are in a state of emotional vulnerability that others will not abuse our trust?

Why do we need to trust? We need to trust because no man, women, or child was meant to live alone. What makes a relationship work is the trust between the individuals who share it. For a bond to be forged, trust must be given and received. For a child to grow into a well-adjusted, positive adult, they must trust and have faith in their journey toward adulthood. People need trust because no one individual is impenetrable, perfect, or can survive by themselves. We long to surround ourselves with those we can relate to, lay down our lives for, and find comfort from in in our darkest hours and on our brightest days.

But is trust something that is given? Is it of the soul? For trust to be obtained, it must first be given, and then received as well. Those who work together out of trust can accomplish much more than those who do so because of greed. Trust is something that lets others know where they stand amongst those in their circle. Trust is what distinguishes acquaintances from family. And it is trust that keeps us whole. At the end of the day, trust, is the most important thing we have. Money is transitory, trends come and go with the times, people move on, but trust in one another lasts for many years. Memories will come and go, and experiences once shared in the heat of the moment will become stories of the past to tell the next generation.

The laughter in times of celebration can easily blind us to the truth of what we fight for. Victory and times of peace can make us forget those whom we stood side by side with on the battlefield. Yet trust is what can bring us back to our comrades after so many years apart. The king seeks trust above all things, even gold. It is trust that makes him have more faith in those beneath him than those born into a higher social status. It is trust that is more precious to him than the enemies conquered, resources gained, and allies won.

Trust, rather than what we know or have gained over time, is the one thing that can make us equal. Though a brotherhood and a sisterhood may be founded on social commitment, trust is what allows the commitment to flourish. Trust is the one thing that reminds us of who we are to others in times of adversity. It is all that keeps us together and it makes us stronger. How can one say there is love among them when there is no trust to begin with? Even thieves need trust. Even enemies value trust. Even those who have known nothing but lies and deceit value trust. What are we if we do not trust each other?

For what are we without trust?

CHAPTER 7

LOYALTY

oyalty, the one thing that commands respect amongst all people and all species of life that exist within the natural and physical realm. Of all the things I've studied, loyalty is the one thing that all people seek. It is the validation of the judgement in the eyes & psyches of others as to determine the validity to the truth that each person professes.

I find it amazing that some words that are short in length, are the most meaningful in people's lives. I find it amazing that human beings can lead a mundane existence and have only a superficial understanding of the world around them, yet create words based on concepts that define us, (whether aware of them or not). Love is something we all desire, and loyalty maintains love. If it is trust that can bring people closer than expected, it is loyalty that keeps them together. Loyalty is an admirable quality. Like all things not contained within the realm of money, loyalty is something all heart's desire and all minds crave because it cannot be bought.

Loyalty, a quality that people live and die for. Loyalty, can shape the reality of a person's perspective. Whether on the job, at home, or in a relationship, it is loyalty that all people desire. It is loyalty that keeps the friends we have close to us. It is the loyalty from those we trust that keeps us going through the hard times. What is a brotherhood, a sisterhood without loyalty? What is a nation if it is not loyal to its populace? What is a marriage if those who come together before their creator are not on the same accord? We all want to be surrounded by those who are loyal to us, faithful to us, in agreement with us. We all want to be with those who come to us of their own volition and go to lengths for us that they would not go to for others. We all want to be loyal to those who are loyal to us. We want it because trust can come and go, but loyalty is what makes us stay.

It is in loyalty that we find the faith to be with the person we have committed our lives to. It is in loyalty that a brother is accepted amongst those who he calls brother, and it is in loyalty that a sister is accepted amongst those she calls her sister. A strong oath, a strong bond will be upheld by those who remain loyal to it in all things they do. It is loyalty that drives our existence. It is the journey toward loyalty that, among other things, drives the very essence of human interaction. Once we are equipped to survive the conditions we live in, we seek to form bonds with those we live among. Not just any bonds, but genuine bonds. Bonds that no man can touch. Bonds that no matter the life circumstance, will stand the test of time and will never waver. The human soul innately seeks loyalty in kindred spirits in a land of strangers, foreigners, and lost souls. It is loyalty that gives the soul a sense of calm and clarity in life. It is the loyalty, the strength, the support from others in this land of the lost that gives us a sense of ease. Genuine loyalty is sought by all people from all walks of life. Its availability makes it that much more of a blessing in the eyes of those who seek it. And it is what loyalty is based on that we fight for it with our very last breath.

What does it mean to be loyal? I have seen how people justify their actions out of loyalty. I have seen the lengths that people will go to remain loyal to the ones they love. Loyalty is a treasure reserved for all, yet we are all guilty of sometimes becoming blind to its meaning. Some believe loyalty can be bought, like a commodity. Some believe loyalty to be a weapon used to further their own interests. When I observe people around me, I see that we all hold loyalty to different degrees. We hope those we open up to will not take advantage of our kindness or the lengths we will go to prove how much they mean to us. To those who value loyalty from an emotional or spiritual perspective, we want loyalty to come from the heart. So many try to find good things in this twisted world. We try to find light in darkness, order in chaos, peace in times of war, and loyalty in a place governed by infidelity.

Yet many of us never stop to ask ourselves, what it means to be loyal. Does loyalty mean to having an unwavering sense of duty or commitment to those we trust? Does being loyal mean that we will heed their call no matter the circumstances? Does it mean bearing the burden of our trusted brethren when they have committed an act outside of their moral code that we may not agree with? Does being loyal mean that we will always deliver on our word? Does it mean that loyalty is then based on actions? For what is the benchmark of loyalty? What determines whether a person is loyal in the eyes of strangers? I have seen how people interact when their relationship is grounded in loyalty. I have seen how people of different races can come together, be friends, and remain so throughout their lives. It is not money that keeps them together, not what goods and resources each brings to the table, it is loyalty. Time after time, I have seen groups of people stay close with one another. The times may change, those around them may change, even they themselves may change. But even after years apart, it is the strong friendship maintained through loyalty that makes it seem as if they were never apart.

When we look at the world, we see alliances among countries. We see how it is the goods and resources that keep one from destroying the other. Yet so many wonders what happens when that alliance falls apart. Will war start? How many innocent lives will be sacrificed for one country's greed? How many innocent souls will become stained with the blood of those who were never apart of the conflict? To what extent will the boundaries of loyalty be pushed? How would such an event test a soldier's loyalty to their nation? Could they kill on the orders of those who have never taken a life? Could they live with the guilt, the shame, the screams, the nightmares, the depression, the carnage of war because they choose to be a good soldier and remained loyal to the ideals and principles of their nation? Could they fight a war that never needed to happen, all because of loyalty? Could they return home the same person, look their loved ones in the eye and not destroy all that they love, all because of loyalty? Could they fight for their country when it contradicts their doctrine, all out of loyalty? Could they be the harbingers of death, all because of their loyalty to their nation?

For what good is loyalty, if you will never know what it means and where its boundaries lie?

What good is loyalty, if one knows what it is they truly sacrificed?

Should there be a border, a boundary put in place to remind us of the limits of what we will do or how far we will go for another person? Does a person contradict themself when they put their level of loyalty to another person or a group in a box? Does such a decision lead to anger, resentment, suspicion, mistrust amongst a group of people when their level of loyalty is not absolute? In social groups such as the Church, the Knights Templars, fraternities, sororities, gangs, or any social unit with a goal, each member takes an oath they are expected to uphold. But at the same time it is assumed that they will also be loyal to those outside the circle. Their loyalty to their cause and their beliefs must be unquestionable. They must act without hesitation and do whatever is commanded. But how far can a practitioner go for loyalty to their faith? If they are conflicted should they question their loyalty to the oath or commitment they have taken? Should they draw a line as to how far their sense of loyalty can be used to justify their actions?

When is it necessary to question one's sense of loyalty to their cause? Does it happen before they go down the path they choose? Or should they do it while they are on the path? Should they do it after they have taken the journey? But anything can happen before, during, or after. So, at what point does one question their loyalty/commitment to what they do? There are times when we must see our endeavors through to the end, and other times when we must question them first. But when do they know when to do so? So many seek a cause to live, a sense of purpose, something greater than themselves to give their time on this earth meaning. So many want to commit themselves to the one thing that brings them the most happiness. Yet a lot of the things that make us happy may not always be good for us. We all want that someone, and that special group of loyal individuals, to call our own. We all want peers who will have our backs no matter what. We all want a hand to reach out from above and pull us up when the waves threaten to drown us. We all want that person who has been there from the beginning, who has been there time after time. We wish for this because it is not money that binds them, but loyalty. And it is in that moment that we realize we have a true friend. A friend who would not sell us out for money or a higher social status but remain loyal to the very end. We all crave someone who will share our burden without question. We know that within that person is the greatest treasure of all. It is a treasure that can move mountains, split the seas, create something that no amount of money can purchase… memories. What is within that person is a reason to live, to keep going, to keep fighting. We know their loyalty is genuine, that it is pure, that it comes from a place that runs deeper than the earth itself.

But what good is loyalty if we do not understand it?

What good is loyalty if it will be the death of us in the end?

What good is loyalty, if it will destroy us in the end instead of being the one thing that made us better when we lived?

Loyalty is something we all need. It keeps us safe, gives us a sense of security, lets us know we are not alone in the world. For each person is one soul surrounded by billions. Within this world is so much confusion, so much chaos, so much war, and so much conflict. Every day is a struggle, every day is a fight just to see tomorrow. Nothing is guaranteed. We tell ourselves that it is, but if it were, life would be different. And to find peace in the war, calm in the storm, hope in disbelief, guidance in the confusion, we look to loyalty. It is the friendly, loyal faces of those grounded in the same beliefs we hold that gives comfort us and give us a desire to make it through another day. Whether friend, family member, religious organization, or co-worker, it is that network of loyal individuals who watch over us that gives us reason to see tomorrow. When we extrapolate this concept, it becomes apparent that loyalty is what allows people of all backgrounds to live together in harmony. A bond forged in material things will fade as they fade. But a time-tested bond founded on the principles of character will never lose its strength. It is the loyalty of the people that gives the ruler their power, and it is the loyalty of the ruler whose style of governing seems like a blessing, not tyranny.

For what are we without loyalty?

Will the things we remain loyal to, be the death of us or will they be the things that give us a purpose to live? If so, were they worth it? If not, what was it all for?

CHAPTER 8

FRIENDSHIP

What I would give to relive a memory with my best friends. I remember the fun we had as kids. What made the time spent together fascinating was that we were around people we could open up to without shame, guilt, or embarrassment. If I could turn back the hand of time, and revisit every experience that I once had with my friends, I would. I would watch as his younger self had the time of my life being amongst those I deeply cherished. In some ways it is a shame that with time, we must grow. And as we grow, we lose the childish splendor that made us see our friends the way that we did. If I could, I would cry tears of joy as we fully embraced those moments and forgot about the worries of the world. I would marvel at the fact that we could truly say we are amongst friends, if not family.

We all long for a friend. We all long for someone to love us, care for us, and share our experiences. We desire to be with someone who sees us as we should be. Deep down, we all want to be with someone who will be honest with us when the moment of truth presents itself. From the very beginning, we want that genuine connection. We want to be around someone who is pure in their opinion of us. We all wish to find that person we can call friend. When we are with them, everything we do has a reason, a purpose. When we are with them it is okay to cry, to let out the feelings we suppress and, deny ourselves. It is a good friend who is the shoulder to lean on, to cry on, the face of comfort. When we are with them, there is no storm too hard to endure, no struggle too much to bear. It does not matter if they are near or far beyond the horizon, a true friend is a good friend. It is their company that is our shield. It is their willingness to defend us that is our sword. It is the fact that, despite differences, they are like us in ways we never thought to expect from another person. We all need friends and family because we are meant to be together. It is their smiles, their laughs, their hugs, their kisses, their handshakes, their presence, the times we share, and the memories developed in those moments that comforts us. What we would give to find such a person. For what amount of gold, silver, or any commodity that can be sold be worth in the presence of a true friend? The heart, the human soul desires to find a kindred spirit in a world of unknown faces. Throughout life, we look for people who can identify with us, who can tell us something about ourselves that only we would know. Throughout life we seek to find familiarity in a world where everyone is a foreigner. We form attachments today to help us get through tomorrow, though not all turn out to be genuine. But a friend, let alone those we call family, holds much more importance than we know. It is a shame that all people take for granted their loved ones. We are so deeply governed by the need to survive and meet the demands of the environment that we at times don't treat those closest to us as we should. We never know the true meaning of friendship, or how fortunate we are to have someone, until it's gone or we move on. However, once we are surrounded by our friends, we will never forget the times we share.

I cannot help but wonder, what makes a friend a good friend? Is it the fact that they complete us? Is it that, despite living in a world of different faces and various perspectives, we have a kindred spirit? Is what makes a good friend something genetic or instinctual? Is it because of our defense mechanisms that we automatically look for individuals with traits necessary for survival, and because of that, we befriend them? And the more they can help, the more we call them friend and want to stick by them. We look for something genuine in a person we call a friend. But what makes something genuine? Is it that such a person would not hurt us? Is it that such a person has been neglected by other social groups and will form a social bond with anyone to be part of a social unit? Is it that such a person shares the same beliefs we do? That even when everything is going wrong, they still hold true to the same principles they did when they were on top of the world? Or is it that such a person we call friend really cares for our well-being? Is it that they care for us more than we care for ourselves at times? Is it that such a person truly desires a connection with the person they open to in ways they would not with others? Is it that what they feel for us is not bound to the social plane? That their care and, concern is not grounded in money, power, social advancement, prestige, or a favor to be gained? Is what makes a good friend and someone genuine the fact that their love, for us is not predicated on what we have, what we can have, but for who we are? Is it that a good friend is someone who puts up with our shortcomings, who sees us for who we really are rather than who we present to the world? Is it that a good friend stands by us even when we try to destroy ourselves? Knows the true path for us better than we do? So many think it is the time shared; for others, it is the similar norms. Is it because they see us in a different light than we see ourselves, that they see we can become better than we thought? Is it that such a person will be honest with us? Honest enough to tell the truth, and brave enough to stand by their word? Even when we have accepted the chaos, given into the norms, and conformed to carry on, even when we do not see the light at the end of the tunnel, a good friend stands by us.

But why? What is it about such individuals that compels them to stay when we have given up on who we are, when others before them have left us? For what is it that they believe can be gained when we do not know for ourselves? Such people are so rare and, compelling, they can even provoke our suspicions. For most would leave us now if given the opportunity to move onto someone or something better.

It is funny how you start out. When you get to know each other, it is easy to agree on many things because you are trying earnestly to build a connection with the other person. But as time goes on, the same topics that used to bridge the gap and invoke familiarity are not as easy to come by. And as you grow in your friendship, you wonder how it all began.

I believe that it is our differences that spark a friendship, in places where we least expect it. The King or the Queen can find a kindred spirit from the very people who serve them. The Commander can find a kindred spirit among the lowest soldiers in their ranks. Two enemies, fighting on different sides of a war, can find a bond that they could not with their respective country-men, who have never been in a place wrought with death. I wonder if, in times of war and desperation, the thought of preserving the peace ever kept both sides from spilling any more blood than they already had. Yet in these times, somewhere, somehow, two people were able to put down their biases, their prejudices, and find a common ground. And in fact, it was more than just a systematic alliance and compromise, it was genuine. In that moment, two worlds became one. In that moment, two people became better - in the name of friendship rather than in the name of war.

I find it ironic how opposites attract. For some people, friendships begin because the other has what they desire but lack. For others, it is the desire for a different perspective that makes them pursue their opposite (sort of yin and yang). But no matter how you look at it, people do tend to find friends in places they never though were possible with people they never expected to. I find it a shame that people try to control the realm of friendship the same way they try to control everything else, with logic. In my opinion, friendship goes deeper than logic. Friendship is the spiritual connection of two kindred souls in a place of uncertainty. It is human nature to find a connection with the world that surrounds us. And that is what friendship is, a connection. A connection that is pure, rooted in the heart. It is the longing of all souls. It is why human beings cannot live alone, be alone, function alone, for we were created with the ability to bond with others. To deny such an ability is to be more than lonely; it, is to suffer internally, to no longer live. And when we stop living, we stop being human.

What are friends for?

Who would we be without them?

For in the end, we were not created nor intended to be alone.

The folly, the flaw, the fallacy of human beings when it comes to friendship can be found within the realm of money. We believe money, goods, resources, makes us friends. We believe what can be obtained physically, materially, will only strengthen our bonds. And it is the same things we will fight over that will lead to our demise as friends. We only believe in materialism because the journey to acquire goods, resources, money, whatever, is held in such high esteem in our society. I have come to find that the true strength of friendship is that each group is different from the other. It is the uniqueness of the perspective that each group has that makes each member feel they belong. For if every group believed in the same thing, we would all believe the same thing. But we are not the same. Each of us has a mind of our own, a will of our own, and desires of our own. And while every group believes they know what is best for humanity, it is the uniqueness of each group that allows an outsider to see the various aspects of what it means to be human. In a way, each group shows the other where humanity lies, where it stands, what it represents, yet what it can become. It shows the soul that its perspective is multidimensional. We look for meaning throughout or lives, and find it in our connection with others. And with this understanding, we find a friend.

For time on this earth is hell already, but with a friend, it may be endured.

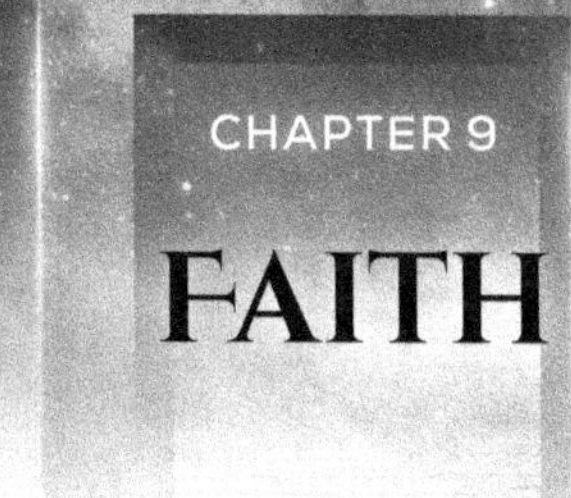

CHAPTER 9

FAITH

What do we know about faith? All we know is that faith is a concept that is both abstract and concrete. It is abstract in the sense that faith goes where logic and reason cannot, yet it is concrete as it shapes the very being of human existence. It guides us, moves us, even if we do not know it. Some equate it with the intervention of divine sources, others see it as a part of being human that is not always logical, but spiritual in nature. It eludes us in the sense that we cannot grasp it the way we grasp the physical world, yet we know it is there. We cannot perceive it the way we perceive the world around us via sensory stimuli from the external environment, yet at its core it defines humanity. It is the feeling one gets when they do not know what to do, yet they are willing to embark on the journey regardless of how things may seem. But what do we know? What do we know of faith?

From the beginning of human existence, people have struggled to understand the dichotomy brought about by faith and reason. If we know so much about faith, why do we struggle so much to accept it? What is it about faith that humanity can never agree upon? How can such an abstract yet concrete concept plagues the mind the way it does, yet shape the future that holds the unknown? How can faith be so abstract that even those deemed rational/logical cannot understand it? They come to the consensus that faith is for those who believe in the divine, yet concrete enough for some of the greatest minds that shaped human history to draw on in their endeavors. How can such a concept hold a philosophical, metaphysical, spiritual, emotional, mental, social, intellectual, and physical dichotomy? How can one concept exist within the human psyche when it goes against the innate cognitive capabilities found within the human intellect? For what do we know about faith? Is their truth, power, meaning in the word? Is there validity, a justifiable claim in its meaning? Is faith a concept that is too much for humans to handle? What do we know about faith other than the meaning given to it by a mind not capable of understanding it? What do we know of its boundaries, limits, parameters? What do we know of its contexts (social, religious, etc.)? What do we know of the word other than its main associations? What do we know of faith outside religion? What do we know of faith outside of spirituality? Is it a concept too much for us to understand within a religious, spiritual context? Or does the concept speak to a part of human nature lost to the modern era? How does one come to know such a term or understand its meaning? Do academic or religious texts offer insight into such a juxtaposed concept? For whom can we say is faithful when they do not understand the complexity of such a term, let alone its two-sided meaning? For what does humanity know of faith when it can never come to common ground on any matter? If humanity lives, faith is both abundant and mysterious to the human psyche.

Of all the concepts known to the human intellect, faith is one of the hardest to fathom, to comprehend because it is not part of human nature. Within human nature is impulse, instinct, intellect, logic, reason, and intelligence, but not faith. It is human nature to look to the known, the perceivable. It is human nature to look at what can be seen, heard, smelled, tasted, or touched. From our bodily senses, the brain maps out an image of the world that surrounds us. From our bodily senses, we live by the physical perceptions that cause us to rely on both intellect and instinct.

Logically speaking, the rational person or the person best geared to survive is the one who relies on their rational and survival instincts. Yet when it comes to faith, such a concept is a contradiction to the rational mind. Why would human beings look to faith rather than their innate reasoning and logical capabilities? Why would human beings choose something that is not part of them (Faith) over something that is (Instinct & Intellect)? Such things make no sense, make one's chances of survival that much harder, cause a person to live a life where they are forever at war with themselves because they are at war with their own nature.

It is hard, especially for the modern being, to trust and have faith in that which is unknown. It is irrational to let things work themselves out when you do not know the outcome, yet have faith that they will work out for in your favor. It is irrational to get into a situation where you do not know all the pieces to the puzzle, let alone have all the pieces. Such a way of thinking, such a way of living does not ensure one's safety and survival in the long term. To the logical, such a way of thinking makes no sense. It does not rely on data, facts, or statistics. There is no reason to it, only emotion. Yet emotion is not a logical response to a situation, but one fueled by primal instinct. To the rational being, what sense would it make to have faith? What logical good comes out of a situation where one must hope that the outcome will work out in their favor? Logically speaking, to have such an outcome, one would have to control, alter, or manipulate the people or the events surrounding a situation to ensure the outcome is in their favor. Those who do so are regarded as strong, and those who cannot are regarded as weak, so incapable of ensuring their own survival that they would stop taking any action and let the situation work itself out. It is easy to see that those who rely on logic, intelligence, and reason, would view those who rely on faith more than their innate cognitive capabilities as weak or unworthy of praise or merit. So weak that they pray or believe that an entity none can see is greater than them, and will somehow deliver them from their weakened state in an illogical manner. At the same time, these people believe that this will make them stronger than those who actually use their innate cognitive capabilities to bring themselves out of their hellish predicament. Thus, many would conclude that those who look to faith, who rely on faith more than logic or reasoning, are weak and do not survive in the end.

From the beginning of civilization, humanity has wondered what the best way is to conduct itself, or what is the right way to be a human being. Some looked to faith, some to the rational. Plenty of good has come from both, yet many are unsure if the two could ever exist together within one being, let alone govern human existence. From the ancient civilizations to the modern ones that have advanced in half the time, faith is still an unknown concept to the individual. Wherever people go, faith goes. It requires something that many believe does not exist within the realm of the living or found within the psychological consciousness of the human being. The ancients believed faith to be something found from a divine source, and that it is by that source that humanity can possess it. Those of the modern era believe faith to be a religious component of a flawed system used to enslave the masses. Others believe faith to be something found within the soul of a human being. Some believe faith is a yearning of the soul to connect with the divine. And it is by faith that humanity can connect with the divine.

What makes faith such a concrete, yet abstract concept is that it has no logical foundation. It is not found within the realm of logic, it is not found within the realm of reason, yet it exists within the earthly realm that is governed by logic and reason. Is one right and the other wrong? Is faith just a concept created to describe the process by which the unknown can be known? Is it the process by which the uncertain can work for people in their favor if they believe it will? Or is there truth, validity, reliability, power in having faith and what it can do? Many struggle with the concept of faith. Many tie faith to an omnipotent, omnipresent, omniscient being by which all things are possible. Many tie faith to what can be if they are willing to take the journey and carry out their endeavors. Even if the path ahead does not result in the desired outcome, the desire itself seems possible.

When I think of faith, I see it as humanity's answer to the question of how the impossible can be possible. I see faith as the path people can take to become better. Many define faith as the complete trust or confidence in someone or something. In a religious sense, faith is the strong belief in God or the doctrines of a religion, based on spiritual apprehension rather than proof. Many accept faith because they believe that within the physical realm exists the workings of a power greater than their own that they call God, regardless of what is discovered by science. Many detest faith because they look to logic and reason and conclude that such a power cannot exist within the physical realm. For the logical, such power does not relate to or fall within the boundaries of science. At its core, faith is a belief in the unknown. When we do not know what will come from a situation no matter how much we look at it, those who rely on faith rather than rationality have hope that things will turn out in their favor. To the logical being, putting faith in a situation that is out of one's control is not wise. Letting the situation work itself out without any say is not always the smartest course of action. Thus, the reason why faith is so hard for human beings to accept is because it makes us give up the control, we would have in a given situation to ensure our survival.

What allows us to venture into the beyond, what allows us to go where none have gone before, what allows us to take a chance on something that others will not, is faith. What allows us to see the journey of the unknown all the way to the end, is faith. Faith is important because faith allows us to go where logic, where reason, will not. What makes the journey of the soul, the pursuit of perfection, the journey to be better in mind, body, and spirit is faith. What makes the fight worth fighting that much more powerful, is faith. What makes all that we do now so that others who come after us may prosper, is faith. Faith is what allows us to be more than what we are. Faith is what allows us to look past science, logic, and proven knowledge, and push towards something that fields of knowledge could not predict before.

When you look throughout history, every revolution, every fight for freedom, every attempt to find the answer that plagues the human mind, is faith. Every point in history that changed humanity for the greater good was one of faith. It is easy to think that it did not take much for such events of the past to shape the world as we know it today, but imagine being in that environment. Imagine being in that point in time, being born in that era where what was accepted was what was unquestioned. Not only that, imagine being the one to challenge the main perspective with the intent to liberate the people, to push humanity forward, yet the one to bear all the criticism that comes with that. What does one do in that moment, cower? Or does one push on with faith that their idea, their contribution, their unique perspective will one day shape the world and push humanity down a better path than it already knows? It is so easy for modern-day descendants to think such a thing because they themselves have never witnessed nor endured such a tipping point in their lives.

It is easy for the children of the modern era to treat such acts of defiance with a batting eye for they are the ones to benefit from those struggles they have never experienced. Humanity, believes science to be the epicenter of its advancement. While such things are true on the surface of the textbooks, it was what laid within the hearts of those made gave such significant contributions to the world where the true story is held. Humanity's greatest strength was never its scientific mind, but what those who believed it could be by way of faith. Whether expressed through the means of science, religion, or politics, it was faith that lead humanity to its sophistication. Where others believed impulse to be the epitome of human nature, others believed it to be love. Where others believed instinct to be the zenith of people, others believed it to be reasoning. Where others thought that man's primitive nature was the only thing he could achieve, others looked to faith. And in looking to faith, they walked by faith. In that walk, what they found was something more than what instinct could produce, what impulse could achieve, and what logic could wrap its understanding around. But such results can only be taken by embarking on that journey. It is only by way of the journey of the soul and the faith to stay on that journey that one can find the answers they seek. It is only by faith that humanity can be more than what it currently is. It is only by faith that can one see what is worth fighting for. It is only by faith that an individual can have the strength, the courage, the will to defy their very being and become more than what they are psychologically, physically, and emotionally meant to be. It is by faith that people can become more than what their innate human nature allows them to be.

For faith is the source of humanity's strength.

CHAPTER 10

PATIENCE

When you think of it, patience is truly a fundamental force that governs the universe. It is a force by which all things in the known world live by and are governed by. It takes patience for the seasons to change, and with it a change in the beginning and ending of life. It takes patience for an unborn life to form within its mother's womb before it is ready to enter this world. It takes patience for the old to become the new and propel the human race into the future. And it takes patience for the new to become old so that the next generation may learn from its mistakes and make improvements where those before them failed. It takes patience for the planets to orbit around the sun, each with its own axis of rotation, each with its own cycle. It takes patience for the most beautiful process to unfold and for the most horrific to occur. Within an ecosystem, each organism has a role, a task it is bred for and completes to ensure the cycle of life. There were no written instructions, yet it would seem to the observer that such instructions were ingrained into its DNA. It is as if no spoken word must be spoken for such occurrences to take place. It is as if each organism knows what to do. It happen of its own accord, when such a process is ready to occur, not when one believes that it is ready to occur simply because they believe so.

For what science calls a fundamental process, to the individual who is of a different perspective, it is called patience. Do we really take for granted these things? Do we truly believe that such things can only be governed by the laws of nature, the methods and theories of science? That there can be no other force that acts upon it? Humanity did not advance overnight. Language, the tongue of common man was not formed overnight. Intelligence was not formed overnight. Sophistication of all the known aspects of humanity did not occur overnight. The marvels that arouse the human intellect to a degree that could only be matched by the minds capable of housing such a capacity did not come overnight. Of all these things, at their creation and at their destruction, patience was there. While we crawled out of the caves of the prisons of our minds, patience was there. It was there when we took our first baby steps, and it is there with us as we dare to venture into the forever unknown void called the future.

The form of a diamond that makes it so rare, the bounty gained from a fruitful harvest, the energy emitted from the sun that gives life to the earth, the delicious dish prepared by the chef, the artful craft of the sculptor, the blissful strokes of the painter, the crafts produced by the craftsman, the discoveries gained by the scientist, the lessons learned by the philosopher, the skill gained by those who seek merit… all of these are achieved by way of patience. Even within the brain, it takes time for synaptic pruning to occur, for electrical signals to pass from the brain to whatever part of the body needs them to survive, for external stimuli to register from our bodily senses into our nervous system. Patience truly does govern the ways of man and the universe.

Of all the virtues most sought after by humanity, patience is the most desirable. It is a simple virtue, yet it can become the essence of one's existence. It speaks to the quality that few individuals possess in a world that is ever-changing. Those deemed patient are looked at as individuals who do not seek to control, but are willing to let life unfold and time take its toll. Some hold the virtue of patience in the highest esteem in human nature, and those regarded as patient are said to be among the epitomes of refined human character. For when one looks at the individual with the character of patience, one cannot help but hold such an individual in a high regard separate from the common individual. It is as if the one of patience has reached a height that those with an impulsive nature could not, has ascended beyond the primitive Though they walk among us, it is as if the patient was not human, but something more.

We ask ourselves how those deemed patient, acquire such restraint, such self-control? How do they manage to not let their instincts get the better of them? What is it they possess that allows them to be so refined, so sophisticated, yet exist in a world bound by primitive human nature? What the ancients called a virtue, modern man calls a characteristic. It is ironic how such a virtue is sought after by beings who gave it is meaning, yet never seemed to acquire it or fully understand it once they did. Why is that? Why give something a name, a meaning, why seek to achieve it, if they can never do so themselves? Does this speak to a lack of understanding of such a virtue? Or is it that its creators do not understand it as much as they think they do? For what is the price to be paid for basking within the realm of patience? How sweet is it to the touch? How soothing is it to the soul who has at long last acquired it? Does it taste like pure honey straight from the honeycomb? Are its nutrients those of the natural herbs replenish the ever-dying human body? How can one who will never know its true embrace ever know its touch? Of all the virtues sought after, patience is the most elusive. It is forever within our grasp; we just do not know it. It eludes us because we think we know what it takes to obtain it. Patience eludes us because we think we can acquire it the same way we acquire most goods. Patience eludes us because we think that once we have it, we no longer must work to understand it or maintain it. When I think of patience, I think of a piece of the human puzzle that allows humanity to put all the other pieces together. Without that piece, the puzzle will never be solved, and the big picture will never be realized. It is the folly of human thinking to believe that one's wishes will be granted when one wants them to. It is foolish of an individual to think that life is based on the terms and conditions they want it to be. Every time we think we are ready, we fall short. At times we barely make it. When we think that we have what it takes, the situation shows us a different result than the one we hoped for.

Has such a virtue been lost to the ages? Have the modern generations that have advanced in half the time that it took for ancient civilizations to do so lost such a virtue that comes with time? Has their level of advancement and sophistication made them forget the virtue that all things within their realm of existence abides by? Has patience become a relic of the past to the current generation, though it is more basic than virtues of the future may be? Has humanity lost its desire to be better than its baser instincts, and reduced patience to something used only for mundane?

What is patience? Is patience just a concept used to describe something that is not within our nature? Is it something that can only be achieved by seeking our higher character? Is patience a virtue? A virtue that was used to embark on a journey to develop one's character? Is it a right that belongs to all people that make up humanity? Is patience something that is mandatory for each person to have? Is patience how all things become better? Does it take patience to grow into the man or women we will one day become? But who is to say that each person will develop patience to the same degree and that each situation they go through will make them a patient person? Is patience something we learn from gaining an understanding of certain intricacies in life? Does one learn patience from the understanding that all things or nothing, are not within our grasp? Does one learn patience from the understanding that we are not as powerful, as knowledgeable as we imagine ourselves to be in our psyches? Is patience learned from the understanding that we are not ready and that we will never be ready? Does it come from the understanding that for all our worth, all our obtained knowledge, all our worldly possessions, we are forever in an imperfect state? Does patience come from the understanding that the physical realm and its beings are forever flawed? Flawed in the sense that because they live in the world of the material, they will always change due to the demands imposed by their environment? That no matter what they create or, fathom, once they put it into the physical realm, it will be imperfect? But even though it is imperfect, with time can it become better? Is patience derived from that knowledge?

Is patience derived from the understanding that while we will never be perfect, the things we create will never be perfect, they can become better with time? Is patience a virtue of our higher selves? Is patience an inkling of the soul? Is patience the soul's way of communicating to our conscious minds that we are not in control? That this illusion of the ability to manipulate the natural course of events will be our downfall? Is patience the soul's yearning to stop us from going down the path we deem best when we are not yet ready to do so? Is patience the yearning of the soul to understand that with change comes time, and with time comes understanding? And once we have understanding, are we ready to take the journey that we were at one point in time not ready to take? Does this virtue come by way of the development of our individual character? Will every person who has developed their character acquire patience?

Patience. It defines a person in ways that only such a virtue can. It defines an individual in a way that nothing else can. Patience, why have it? Why need patience when one possesses logic and reasoning? Why have patience when one can calculate, quantify, exploit, examine, and categorize the world around them? Why look to patience as it relates to character when all one's primitive nature thinks about is survival? Those thoughts are innate, but is patience? Or is logic and reasoning something that comes by acquiring the virtue of patience? Is patience within human nature? From a certain perspective, patience is possible to achieve, yet it comes by way of a journey to reach self-perfection or refinement of one's own nature. But is that a journey all individuals at one point in their life are willing to embark on? Is patience something that everyone wants to obtain in their lifetime? Therefore, is patience the same for everyone?

The young have much to learn. That is why they need patience. For they are headstrong, bold, energetic, yet aloof to the ways of the world and themselves. The old have much to reflect on as they educate the young. They may be wise but can no longer bear the strains of life that they could when they were blessed with youth. Each can learn from the other, but it takes time, and with time comes patience. With time comes change, with change comes dilution, and with dilution comes perspective. For the young can learn from the old, and the old can teach the young. As it relates to humanity and its character, it is by way of patience that peo-ple can become more than what they are. If faith is what gives people the belief that they can be better, it is through patience that they can do so. It takes patience to be a husband. It takes patience to be a wife. It takes patience to raise a child into the adult they will one day become. It takes patience to turn weakness into strength, but even more patience to understand what that means. With patience comes skill. With patience comes form. With patience comes knowledge. With patience comes understanding. The irony of patience is that it does not choose us, we choose it. And if we do not choose patience, patience chooses us. The ignorant remain so because they choose to live within the realm of their limited perspective. The arrogant remain so because they let their belief in their over inflated self-importance consume their psyche. And the impatient remain so because they choose to neglect the virtue of patience. Yet, patience is like any women; it does not need us, want us, desire us. However, if you work for her affection, if you prove your worth to her, you come to the understanding if she desires you (which comes with patience). But you are willing to work in order to feel her love and her gaze; she will accept you and make you better than the man you once were.

Patience is like the wave at sea that lets you set sail off into the unknown. You will never know when such a wave will hit your vessel, but when it does, you must be ready. For when it hits you, it will propel you that much closer to your destination. You must be patient and trust that it will guide you when it deems that you are ready for the journey that lies ahead. Patience is important for it is a virtue. Nothing good ever came from the one who believed themselves to be ready for a journey they did not know of. Nothing good ever came from rushing a process that takes time. Patience is the way by which character is developed. Patience is the way by which an individual can become better than they once were. For when we are ready, we are not. For when we are willing, we are not sure. For when we believe ourselves to be ready for the road that lies ahead, we are ignorant of what it entails. But with time we acquire patience, and once we have patience, the true journey begins. Patience. For it is a virtue, perhaps the most misunderstood. It is only when you take the journey for yourself that you understand what it is. It is only when one takes the journey toward connecting with their soul that they will they come to understand what can be found in patience. For patience is a word, yet it is a force by which all things live and breathe. It is a way of life by which all things thrive. It is so much more than we even know. It is only by living our life that we can obtain it, and understand who we are in relation to it and how it affects our lives. For patience truly is the key to all things, and it is patience that can unlock all doors, but with time.

CHAPTER 11

UNDERSTANDING

We go through life trying to make sense of it all: the who, the what, the when, the how, the why. We try to find meaning in the time, the era, the situation, and its circumstances. Through life, we try to make sense of our existence. We try to understand ourselves, our nature, our character. We try to distinguish ourselves by our traits, our faults, our flaws, our shortcomings, our experiences with the goal of coming to terms with who we are. We articulate our perspectives as we believe that ours are right and others wrong. We compare to know where we stand with those around us.

Some look to the spiritual to understand the essence or the inner most depths of all things. They take a journey. A journey that delves deep into their spiritual nature. It questions us on a philosophical level, getting to the very core of what it is we all seek to know. We desperately want to know the inner workings of what we cannot see. We want to know the complexity that makes us up the reality that is captured through our senses. We want to go to the place, the realm, the depth that science cannot. We want to know these things because we believe it will help us understand ourselves, our nature, who we are, why we do the things we do, why we treat ourselves and others the way we do.

For us, a sense of understanding answers the existential question of our being as well as our existence. It gives clarity to a mystery that has plagued us since we walked the vast yet limited miles of the earth's surface. We believe that the old have it and that the young venture toward it on the quests that can only be taken because of their youth. But as we get older, we realize that no one ever truly has understanding. As we get older, we become more familiar with it. To say that one has it, is to say that one has lived. To say that one truly possesses understanding makes them seem something more than those we live amongst. To make the claim that one has it in its entirety is to say that such an individual is farther from the path than they believe themselves to be. From the tales of the wise we learn that it is only by taking a lifelong journey that one may obtain true understanding. Legends and myths tells us that it is by embarking on heroic quests that the heroes and warriors may seek it. For to obtain such a thing as understanding is rarer than any handheld treasure that any man, women, or child can have. For this one thing that cannot be held, touched, tasted, smelled, or seen is more desirable than anything else. Wars have been fought over it. In the quest for understanding, nations have crumbled yet been built stronger than ever, people have been made whole and their purpose made clear.

With understanding, the most uncanny and mysterious dichotomies of life become nothing more than a lessoned learned. It is by the blessing of this fundamental force that all things become clear. It is by this fundamental principle that one truly becomes a master. It is only by living that we acquire it. And it is only by way of the journey of the soul that we come to know it more and more. For the wise are claimed to have understanding, and the old find comfort in it as they age each day. One can say that the more one lives, the closer one grows to it. What could be more powerful than knowledge? What can be more powerful than power? What can have more worth than gold? What makes solving a mystery or riddle worth the cognitive effort? What gift can sooth the soul other than understanding? What makes life that much more bearable than the lies we tell ourselves and others simply because we do not know the answers? What can be more important than the one thing we live for? The sages of old thought it to be the one thing worth living for. The religious sects of old thought it to be the answer to knowing the divine on the most spiritual level. To them, it was by way of this, by seeking this one fundamental principle, that life in its fullest became clear. To them, it was reaching an understanding that they could achieve all things.

We go through life trying to find understanding. In all that we do, we try to understand the why. Why do we do it? Why do we need it? Why do we want it? Why do we feel this way? Why do we see things the way we do? Even in the smallest spaces of our minds, we ponder the meaning behind all things, whether we find them bothersome or fulfilling. We want to know the forces at work that govern the situation that produces the action. Whether in psychology, politics, astronomy, physics, law, culture, religion, philosophy, fashion, government, we try to find the way.

When one looks at the different fields of study, one cannot help but wonder why, so many were created to understand man. Was it to expand his empire? Was it to expand his ways, his teachings, his ideas, his norms? Or was it to understand the complexity, the dichotomy that is his nature? For in all things lies a meaning. For in all things, there is a force that governs its conception. Throughout life we try to find where exactly understanding can be found. Can it be found within the crevasse of one's mind? Can it be found amongst others? Does it come by way of conversation between two or more individuals exchanging ideas and thoughts about what they believe to be true and not true? Is it found within the individual? Does it take a person to deeply reflect upon themselves and their experiences to find the understanding of their life spent on earth? Every day we think about it yet never find it. Some rarely question it as it is normal for them to do so.

Some come to believe that they have already found the answers they seek and have come to an understanding of themselves that warrants no further investigation into their soul. Yet as we live, we lose sight of it. We become so entranced by the world that we live in, so put down by the constant demands of life, so blindsided by the continual information that we take in everyday from the world around us that we lose touch with the understanding that we have come to obtain. We can never understand it entirely but treat it as something that will last forever. It is our ego that prevents us from truly reaching it. It is the pride in our achievements that blinds us to its true meaning. It is our very nature that limits us from becoming one with it. It is our arrogance that blinds us to the true perspective that it offers. It is the lies we tell ourselves that hinders us from accepting the truth(s) that understand brings. It is our fleeting ambitions that lead us to believe that such a journey to obtain understanding will allow us to last forever. For when we are young, we are bold. However, when we are young, we are stupid. We are so stupid that we never realize how little we know and understand. It is such arrogance and such ignorance that lead to our downfall.

It is because of our meager creations that we believe we are right and can never be wrong. Our limited perspective leads us to believe that all that comes from our hand can never do us harm and that reinforces what little intelligence we have. But it is as we age that we understand that we are not as invincible, smart, cunning, refined as our youth lead us to believe. It is only as we age that we understand that our perspective is subject to the same faults as we are. It is only as we age that we understand we are just as easily manipulated, coerced, limited, and stupid now as we were back then. It is only as we age that we understand that what we thought we had, we never had at all. And because we never did, we never understood it for what it was and could never see it for what it could be. And it is only when we are old, that we understand this truth. Therefore, the old are wise and the young are dumb.

What is the price of such a treasure? What does it take for an individual to have understanding? Must they go through their own hardships? Must they endure as other have endured? Must they suffer as others have suffered? But what toll will such hardship impose on them? Who is to say that they will learn what a situation demands them to learn? How does one know that such a hardship will make them a better person? How will anyone know whether the trials that life brings about will teach them the necessary lessons needed to make them a better person? Why is it that no matter the date, the age, the point in time, the era, the millennium, each generation makes the same mistakes in a different way? Why is it that as a whole society we can never come to the same understanding? Is it that the one thing all individuals prize and fight for (free will) is the one crutch that limits us from coming to the same understanding? Is it that regardless of the generation, there will always be a need for a new perspective that challenges old one? How does one know when to question the ways set by the old and abide by them? When do people know when to drift away from the old ways and establish new ones? With this difference in perspective, how do we come to a universal understanding? Why is it that understanding is viewed differently for all people? Even within one's own nation, there are differences among the same populace. Why is that?

Even if one's ideology is unique, others will always see it in a different way. Throughout history, that has always been a good thing. It has allowed some to speak up against a rule that did more harm than good. It turned a leader into a dictator, a king into a tyrant. It led to atrocities in the name of a faith that was not their own. Yet with time came a new perspective. And with this change in how one originally sought what was and what was not, they lost touch with the core things that made them human… their soul and spirituality. And we all suffer now because of it. For what is understanding but our own unique interpretation of what it is? What is understanding if we only know what it is on our death bed? What is understanding when we spend our whole life trying to seek it, only to have it but for a few short moments? For how can we say we know it if we are too stupid, too limited, too rational, too scientific? Are we so blind to the concepts and the constructs that we once looked to for existential meaning that we no longer look to them for guidance? Are we so disconnected from our primitive nature that we forget how much we are fueled by the instinctual nature to survive? Have we alienated ourselves from our spiritual nature, our own spiritual depth, so much that we no longer look for a deeper meaning in anything outside of science? Have we become so sophisticated that there is nothing left for us to explore? Have we become so refined that the very things that have conflicted humanity for so long no longer conflict us? Is there truly no need for an individual to seek understanding in their lives? Are modern generations, so scientific, so rational, so engulfed by the physical plane of existence that they no longer deem it a necessity to understand the dichotomies, the intricacies, the complexities of our own nature? Have we become so engulfed in the limited world of our own creations that we no longer deem it necessary to delve into the one thing that doesn't have an end, but is a bottomless pit of unquantifiable and unfathomable depth… our soul?

Why is understanding a need of the heart? Why is understanding a yearning of the soul? Because it is who we are. Humans see themselves as the epitome of all things. We see ourselves as the zenith of all creations yet fail to understand what that means. With time, our creations have gotten the better of us. They led us to believe that we are incapable of being at fault or erring in judgement of character. They led us to limit our own perception of our existence, and trap us in the realm of what we already know. With victory, we lost sight of what once was, deeming it irrelevant and a thing of a failed era.

But with time came advancement, with advancement came technology, and with technology came sophistication. We came to believe that with the sophistication of the environment and our living conditions came sophistication of the soul. This belief led us to the certainty that we are the end all be all. It led us to believe that there is no end to our accomplishments and no limit to what we can reach. And that the journey of the soul is a mundane one. We believe that understanding is academic in nature when it is indeed spiritual at its core. Knowledge comes from texts but understanding comes from living life. Understanding is important because it lets us know what we truly possess which is spiritual, not materialistic in nature. When we understand what we possess, we understand that it is never housed in money, goods, and resources. It is found within us. Its resides within the soul, the individual, the people, each nation, the future generations to come. Understanding is the uniqueness each will bring to right the wrongs of those who came before them.

It is the contributions each generation brings to humanity to make it more than what it once was. For what we have is not limited to the resources we possess but to the ingenuity found within the imaginations of our mind which reflect our soul. What we possess lies in the heart. It's the faith, the will, the courage, the yearning of the soul to be better, to be more than what those before us were. It is the potential, the power, the ability to be better. But how does one take the journey to find understanding? What does it take to understand it at its core? For even when we think we have it, do we? When will we know if we have it or not? Will we ever come to know what we have once we do? Will we ever know it definitively? How do we begin the journey? One day at a time.

With time comes patience. And with patience, comes understanding.

If knowledge is power, then understanding is mastery.

CHAPTER 12

EMOTION

What separates man from the machine? What separates human-ity from the very things it creates? What separates those who care from those who do not? What is it that makes people, people? What makes a lover love? What makes the scientist think in ways misunderstood to those around them? What is it that truthfully brings people together? What is it that allows people from worlds apart, cultures apart, generations apart, religions apart, ages apart, ideas separate from their own come together in a way that is unexpected yet innate to human nature? What truly makes a mother, a mother? What makes a father, a father? What makes raising a family have that much more meaning behind it? What gives all that we do meaning? What makes all that we have hold meaning to our hearts? What is it about caring, having a heart, that means something? What makes a revolution so instrumental to human existence? What makes freedom of thought deadly to the ideas it threatens yet so powerful to the people who possess it? What makes one stand firm in the face of the unknown? What makes all that we do mean something? What makes caring worth it? What makes us trust a total stranger more than we trust those we have known our whole lives? What makes every action that we take worth it? What makes every outspoken word that frees us from the bondage that enslaves us have such meaning? What makes humans, human?

What makes man, man? What makes the compassionate, passionate? What makes those who stand up for what is right because it is right hold so much meaning to those who live on to tell their tales to the next generation? What makes someone emotional? What makes the time spent with others, one's experiences, the challenges and trials overcome hold significance to us as we get older? What makes the love a man makes to a woman connect him to her soul? What makes the love a woman has for a man make him go out of his way to love her in ways he never thought he was capable of? What is it that allows humanity to venture into what it once called the unknown and advance itself in ways it thought foreign to its primitive nature? What is it that truly governs humanity and the human existence? What is it that fuels us, governs us, gives us passion, gives us power, potential, greatness? What is the strength that humans truly possess? What is the source behind the greatness of the marvels, advancements, sophistications, achievements, monuments that humans worship for years and years to come? What is it that makes praise to the divine so powerful that it can be heard from the deepest crevices of the earth to the highest heights of the heavens? What gives meaning to us tiny humans, with our limited intellect, our limited perspective, trapped within our own little bubbles, intertwined with those of others we interact? What is the one thing that humanity thinks it understands but truly does not? What is the depth that many scholars have discussed but has never been understood by the masses? What is the very thing that governs us, connects us, blinds us, yet we never see nor truly understand? What is this thing we keep questioning with the intent to understand, but never can? What is, this one thing we think we know so much about yet are so consciously and unconsciously controlled by it that we can never understand it because of its most intimate nature?

I say It Is Emotion

What is Emotion?

Human beings truly are the divine's most contradictory creations. In one vessel, you have intellect, physicality, emotion, and spirituality. While each is a domain of its own, each comes together to govern one individual. Yet of all the domains, what governs humanity the most is its emotional spectrum (which is tied to its spirituality). The emotional spectrum. Within it, one finds the very essence that governs the human soul. It is the very component of the human being that gives meaning to all their encounters and experiences. It is by way of the emotional spectrum that one finds the definitive difference between man and machine. It is the one characteristic that separates the cold-hearted calculations made by the most hardened of hearts from the impulsive yet moral decisions of those who are not governed by logic.

The emotional spectrum. While it has been studied by scholars of the old and the new, one can never truly understand how such a domain can exist and govern an individual who possesses the opposite of such a spectrum… logic and reasoning. While opposite from the realm of logic and reason, emotion is somehow intertwined with it. You cannot have one without the other, and to negate one is to be imbalanced. When an individual seeks to acquire knowledge while forsaking their emotions, they become less human. And in doing so, they lose the one thing that makes them human. No matter how hard humans run from their emotions or negate them, they can never outrun the one thing that truly governs them.

What I have come to find interesting about emotion is how opposite it is to logic. Logic is predictable in that it follows a particular pattern of thinking and events that take place in an organized fashion. Conversely, the emotional does not care for order and focuses only on feeling, rather than critical thinking, therefore making it unpredictable. While the logical has a set way by which it can do things, the emotional has a unlimited and unexpected way of governing how a person responds to an act depending on the emotion that they feel: The tears of pain, the tears of happiness, the weight of guilt, the shame brought by guilt. The eruption of joy, the abundance of happiness, the nostalgia of revisiting peaceful memories. The events brought about by anger, rage, frustration. The excitement brought about by anticipation. The inability to act due to fear, the relentless beating of the individual that comes with doubt, the willingness to fight because of love. The tears of pain that come with shame, the pride that comes before the fall because of envy. The loneliness that comes with sadness. The ever-warming security that comes with trust. The things we love the most taken from us because of the hatred that consumes our hearts. The horror that comes from crossing a line we thought we would never cross. The admiration we have for those we respect. The feelings of adoration for the things we love and hold dear to our hearts. The anxiety we get when we try to predict and calculate with the intent to overcome the unknown. The sense of awe we feel when basking within the presence of that which is greater than our senses and that gives us a sense of transcendence. The sense of romance as we seek to be with the one we love. The empathy we feel as we relate to those who have been where we have been emotionally. The sympathy we feel in our desire to help those who need it. The sense of satisfaction we feel when we have had our fill. The sexual feelings we feel in the heat of passion and intimacy. The gratitude we feel for those who help us when others would not. The hope we have when we think about the future and what it could be.

Those of a "sophisticated nature" shun emotion as they believe it to be the downfall of human nature. They see it as the opposite of critical thinking (which it is). Yet I see emotion as part of our intelligence that is tied to the genius allowing us to strive for the unknown, or that which only the individual can seek. It is how one feels about a field of study, a topic of interest that allows one to explore it in a way only they can. Emotion is the joy of basking within it in a way that speaks only to us, that allows creativity, ingenuity, innovation to take hold. It comes by way of a childish imagination and a playful spirit. It allows a singular individual to take something so complex, something developed by the work of advanced minds, and render it comprehensible to the simple-minded. At the very conception of genius, if one looks closely, emotion gathers. It gathers within one who holds it close. It is the love cherish that allows them to explore it in a way that others could not. While logic is for idiots, creativity is for geniuses.

Those who have sophistication see emotion as something that makes people weak when, in fact it is our very strength. Emotion reminds the individual that what they feel is real. Real in the sense that it bothers us, shakes us to our very core. It moves us in a way that logic cannot, and reminds us of our limits, our boundaries, what we can accomplish. It reminds man that he is not all powerful. It reminds man that he is not invincible. It reminds man that there is a line that even he will not cross. It reminds us that we are only human. It gives us the ability to feel, to sympathize, to empathize, to have compassion, to have courage, to have hope. It allows us to feel what most organisms cannot. It allows us to dig deep into our core and see the events that take place in a way that logic cannot. It gives us a sense of attachment. An attachment to what we deem special to us, sacred to us, precious to us. It allows us to care for what we have to a degree that we could not when neglecting what is to be discarded. It allows an individual to fight in a way that those not fueled by emotion could not. To live, to draw breath, to experience life, to move, to interact, to long for, to yearn for, to have that which you can hold, to have that which you can feel, to have that which you can cherish, to have that which you can call your own, to obtain that which your heart desires, is to have emotion.

To the "sophisticated being" (one that prizes intellect over anything else), an emotional reaction is the response of a lesser being, yet to the simpleton, emotion is all that governs us. It is seen as someone who is not of a refined intellect or character; yet to the simpleton, expressing emotion is the very thing that gives all that they do a sense of purpose. However, the emotional spectrum is a realm within its own. If it is not governed by the principles that govern logic, then what is it governed by? And if the emotional spectrum is not understood in the same manner as logic, how is humanity ever to comprehend its true depths? For how does one understand the opposite? On one hand, how do we understand a component of ourselves that is the opposite of the one thing that consciously and unconsciously controls us? And on the other hand, how do we understand another component that has the same function but operates in a different way (subconsciously and consciously)?

Nothing will never be done without emotion. Men can hide from it, women can ignore it, children may never understand it, but emotion will never die. For as long as there is attachment, there is emotion. If there is a yearning, a feeling, a desire, there will always be emotion. To the individual of the era, emotion will always be there. It is what lets a man be a husband, and a woman a wife. It is what makes a human a human and not a machine. It what gives a leader a connection to their people and makes their rule true and just, and not a reign. Emotion is what makes all that is done meaningful. For it is in emotion that humanity can go past the logic, the reason and push toward something greater. For emotion is the part of the human being that allows man, women, and child to go past what is logical and to where wonders become reality. It is what allows the right thing to be done instead of the logical thing. It is what makes people take a stand for what is right because it is right. It is what allows revolutions to occur, the people to sidle up and fight for their country. While people may struggle with this aspect of their nature, the worst they can do is run from it or suppress it. The intellectual will always see emotion as something that is weak, or maybe it is they who have not journeyed to reach their own soul. But to the true, the just, the triumphant, it is emotion that paves the way. Nothing that changed the course of human history for the greater good came by way of being logical. It is the greatest gift ever bestowed upon man. Emotion, the ability to feel is knowing that our days are numbered, yet while we live, our time spent on the planet has some meaning. Knowing that as we age, as we grow, as we learn, we live, and as we live, we feel, and as we feel we become the one thing we try our best to run from… being human. I find it ironic that we run from the one thing we dread the most, yet it governs us in a way that we may never understand. We fear because actions taken out of emotion do not always do us any good. Yet is that because of our emotional state, or the lack of time we spend with ourselves to understand it and how it makes us do that which we deem desirable or undesirable? It makes one wonder, if there is a divine creator, why did such a being so complicated create us in a way that is so contradictory in every way? Why give us logic and reason only to put within us emotion and spirituality? Does it speak to the creator itself? Does the creation reflect the creator? Will we ever know?

Emotion, the one thing we run from. But the more we run from it, the closer we get to it.

CHAPTER 13

GUIDANCE

At conception begins the creation of a life that will grow to be unique. Such uniqueness, such a perspective specific to that life can be the idea that shapes humanity for eons to come. Yet no one knows their purpose, their goals, their visions for themselves at a young age. Such aloofness can prevent an individual from taking the journey of self for themselves, hindering their potential and never allowing them to realize the true extent of their greatness. So, what do we do? We create standards, ideas, concepts, guidelines, ideals that will bring out of us what we could never achieve on our own. We look to that which is greater than us to help us become the epitome of ourselves in a realm of existence that is small in its totality, yet large to us for we are unaware of anything outside and inside of ourselves. In our attempt to understand why we fall short, why we are so powerful yet fragile, we discover that like many other things we are prone to distractions of the senses. The moment we think we have conquered what were once the chains that held captive our freedom, we have been conquered by illusions of our own victory. The moment we believe we have reached what we deem the ultimate level, we become that much more engulfed in our own ignorance, which further enlarges our own arrogance. And if we ever become aware of the uneasiness of our soul, which allows us to reflect, will we ever ask ourselves, what is it we lack?

Philosophy, religion, spirituality, worldliness, the ideas that governs the hearts of man, moves the hearts of women, and influences the imaginations of children. As we enter this world, we know nothing but the care of our parents or the cruel lessons we learn on our own about people and society. We take what we can by adopting the good and learning about the bad while trying to find out who we are underneath the skin. Looking inward, an individual seeks to know about themselves what cannot be learned from others. For there are many places to learn, many lessons to learn, many epiphanies we try to reach before we enter a self-absorbed world, all with the intent to be prepared for what we will have to face on our own someday. As intelligent as we are, we still fall short. In this world of our own creation fueled by our own imagination, we are still limited. As much as we would like to believe that we are the epicenter of our own success, there is much we must be taught. For who can say that they are the end all, be all of themselves? Who can say that all they have achieved they owe unto themselves? Who can believe that their own merit is all because of their own capabilities? It is easy to believe that when we have reached our goal, all that has transpired, all that has happened, is because of our own actions.

Yet when we look back to when we first started, we see that all that we wanted, we lacked. We see that all we needed to get to where we wanted to be, we did not know. For there was a time when we knew nothing of the world, people, even ourselves. There was a time when all we knew were our thoughts, our ideas, the worlds, and concepts we formed in our minds eye, and we doubted even those at some point. It is this understanding that leads everyone to seek the tools, the skills, the knowledge necessary to become their own person. It is the feeling of confusion that stirs within a person that makes them look to others. We seek help to find what we need the most and look to others to push us in a way that only they can respond to. Very few can say that they need guidance. For very few can admit that they are lost, perplexed as to what they seek.

As the child ages, they seeks to surpass the parents. Fueled with the vigor of youth, the energy that seems to come from an abundant source, the onset of puberty and the bodily changes that will propel them to adulthood, they deem themself ready to go beyond the parents. As the student learns, they seek to become the master. The more they learn, the more they implement. The more the student reaffirms their new-found skills and the more their intellect draws them closer to their objective, the more they believe they will possess enough to one day become or even transcend the master. Yet they lack the one component that separates parent from child and student from master… experience. But before they gain experience, they seek guidance. Guidance from those who came before them to help them find what they once sought. Guidance from individuals they hold in high esteem, praised and renowned for their accomplishments and achievements. The downfall of the young is that they are willing to learn, yet do not know how or who to trust to teach them what they really need to know. Such a willingness can propel them to be all that they will one day become or hinder them by fulfilling their desires in all the wrong places. For the love of wisdom is a journey of the soul. Yet how can a person seek guidance in taking a journey that only they can embark on?

As we live, as we try to find our way, we fall. When we think we are ready, we are not. And when we do not want to see if we are truly worthy of what we possess, life will push us into that which will one day forge us into the person we will become. While we all focus on the end of the journey, we never think about how to get there. In our minds, we think it is all figured out, but we never know until we are put in that position. Yet the question remains, how do we get there? How does one find the path meant for them to become their own individual and the epitome of what they can be? There are some things intellect cannot prepare you for, training cannot prepare you for, not even experience can prepare you for. The young are eager to take their place in history by changing the world around them, but how do they know what direction to take? How do they know the path they are on is the right one, but the path for them? For whom is to guide such a mind to achieve one day what those before them never could? Who can be trusted to guide the generations of tomorrow down a path greater than even they know? How does one trust another to be the figure that those who come after them can one day look up to, knowing that such an individual stood the test of time and can be a beacon for future generations to look to as an example?

The hardest part of life is anticipating where an individual will one day stand in the world. We all seek favoritism, a sense of belonging from the masses, but how does one find their way? How does one take the path, the journey to become better in mind, body, and spirit? How does one find guidance in a world that is unfamiliar to a specific individual? How does one find the right guidance in a world that is built on cultures, ideas, and beliefs, but that is fueled and governed by money? How does one find the guidance they need to become their own individual and reach their full potential? How does one find the guidance to one day walk their own path, embark on their own journey of the soul, with the intent to become the epitome of their being, and a blessing unto the world?

What is guidance and where is it found? Is guidance found within religion or in the divine? Is it found within believing in that which is greater than man? Is guidance the yearning of the soul to walk down the path that only it can embark on to become all that it will one day? Is guidance providing the understanding that regardless of what a person has learned or acquired, there are more things they will not know or ever understand? The individual must find direction towards the path that they must walk for themselves with the help of others. Is guidance spiritual in that it pertains to what an individual seeks spiritually, something personal in nature, something specific only to them? Is guidance found amongst others? Others in the sense that no one can reach their destination alone and must seek tutelage from those who once sought what others seek now? Is it a sign of weakness to admit that one is lost and needs help? Is it a sign of weakness to admit that what one thought was the path for them turned out to be something that was never meant for them, and therefore, need a sense of direction to understand their purpose? We know we need guidance but never really know where to look. For the soul yearns for direction as the individual seeks to find their way.

The journey of the soul, the path that all people must one day take to become who they believe themselves to be, where does it start? Does it start at birth? Is it the sole responsibility of the parent to guide their children? But do parents truly understand their offspring? Does a mother know her son, does a father know his daughter? Does a mother truly know her daughter, and does a father truly know his son? Can either parent believe in their hearts that they can guide their child down the path they will one day have to take for themselves? The individual's journey is never set in stone. Unfortunately, society will never come to such an understanding. It will always fail to realize that because each person is different, the guidance they need to become their own person is also different. And it is unfortunate that this guidance cannot be found within the principles of the academic or societal institutions. For some will grow to rule, others to innovate, some to serve, others to fight, others to maintain, some to shape the world to come; each must find the guidance they need.

But what of the mentor? What of the person tasked to care for such a young yet naive soul, to test them, train them, and prepare them to enter a world they know nothing about? Is such a person enough? Can a guardian trust a mentor to propel a child to be all they can become? Can the mentor see the passions of the youth, the vigor and energy? Does the mentor know how best to test it, to mold it into the potential greatness of that specific individual? Is the mentor worthy to be the guiding figure in that individual's life, to put them on the path that they will one day walk for themselves? But who is fit to guide those that will come after? What individual, higher power, human creation, or law/concept that governs the world of man is worthy and willing to guide the hearts of those in the present and of the future? How will one ever know that such people, things, or ideas will ever help guide a person down the path to becoming that which they are in their soul? How will one ever know if the things they commit their life to, if the people in their life, will guide them down the path they are destined to be on?

Why do we need guidance?

Guidance, it is the route to which we seek to understand who we are. Without it, we may never know who we may be if we never dare to venture down the path necessary to become our own individual. No one knows the depth of their soul or what they will one day become, but with guidance, they may walk along the path to one day understand that venture. Every person, everything that exists, needs a way, a method, a process, a force to act upon to make it undergo the change necessary to produce the fruit that it will one day bear. Without guidance, it is lost, and serves no purpose; with it, it may discover its true potential. Without guidance, no person will ever embark on the endeavor that drives them. Without guidance, the greatest minds will never be challenged or mentored in a way that will allow them to go one day where those before them never could. Without guidance, the next generation will never be better than those before them. Without guidance, without principles, without standards, we are nothing more than our primitive nature. Without guidance, we are lost to our own nature. Without guidance, we can never hope to be more than what we are. Without guidance, a boy will never become a man. Without guidance, a girl will never become a woman. Without guidance, a student will never become a master. Without guidance, a sinner will never become a saint. For none that lives knows the way; no one is born knowing which path to take or what their purpose is.

Yet many shun the seeking of guidance. For many believe that to admit that one is lost is the same as admitting defeat. But who know the future? What mortal knows that which has not yet happened? For life is more than what we make it. No matter the journey, the end goal, the point in time, the period in history, we are just as lost now as we were then. For no task is complete; it is only satisfied until it is no longer required. And no human is born knowing the ambition that drives their heart. It is only with time and guidance that an individual will come to such a conclusion.

For without guidance, what are we?

For without guidance, where would we be?

For without guidance, who would we have become?

HONESTY

t is always in short supply. It is lacking amongst the group and in the individual. Underneath all the constructs created to understand that which is foreign and unknown, it gets harder to find. In our attempt to further our own selfish ambitions, we blind ourselves to the objectivity that it will truly set us free. We find it where we want to find it yet ponder when it is not there. We call it what we want to call it in order to fulfill a longing, yet we fall short of it in order to mask our incompetence to those who are lost just as we are. For we fancy ourselves wise when we are ignorant. And we fancy ourselves scholars when we are fools.

Honesty. It is an agreement of sorts. It is a reminder written or a word proclaimed that one will be upstanding with the other. It is an agreement that one will be true to themself. It starts with an accord to find common ground. It begins with admitting one's faults and flaws. It starts by being honorable and truthful about what has transpired. It is a sign of a higher being to admit that which has occurred and recognize the blame each party shares. It is the acceptance in which one faces the intent of their actions as well as its consequences. It is a principle like no other, for its fruit bears more than the words man can create and more than the meaning derived from them. It is a simple thing like all things, yet what makes it impossible is the standard it entails, which we always fall short of. It has no form, no absolute definition other than the one it holds. The only thing that is certain is that it cannot be changed to the liking of the individual who seeks it; if such a thing was true, they would fall short of it. For it is an absolute in a world of change. It is something that will always stay the same, regardless of the many constructs it may take. Yet it is a paradox to the conflicted, the misguided. It is a fallacy to those who have sought truth but denied it. It is a lie to those who never knew what it was they sought for themselves. To the individual who has never come to terms with themself, it is something of their own imagination. To the man of low standards, it is his own defeat disguised as his own success. To those who fashion themselves the epicenter of all, it is their own destruction. An individual who is a follower will never know what it means. Those who never believe for themselves will never know its meaning. The masses will never know of such a force of humankind. Those bound to the ideals of an institution which is not their own will never have it. No matter how hard they try or how much they attempt to force their desired outcome, it will never come to pass. In the end, we will become better because of it, but we will never know it because we are too scared to take such a journey for ourselves. People can never know the meaning such a concept bears unless they take the journey for themselves. Such a thing is not found amongst others, but within us. For if we do not know it in our own hearts, how can we profess it to the minds of others? In a world of darkness, where is the light? In a world of darkness, how can one see the light? In a world whose nature is ever-conforming, where is the strength to overcome it found? In a world of lies, where is the truth? In this never-ending struggle to find something decent, something pure, something that one can call their own, where is the solitude? Where is the isolation? Where is the self? Where is honesty found in the individual?

For how does one describe to the masses in their entirety, honesty? How does one describe to individuals who live by their own sect, their own code, their own religion, their own customs, their own traditions, their own way of life, their own perspective something as complex as honesty?

How does one even know where to begin? How does one begin to converse with others about the benefits of such a virtue and such a longing of the heart? How can those whose lives are found on subjectivity comprehend, let alone live according to, something that is objective? Yet how does the individual who is lost to its ways come to understand its meaning? How can those lost be found? How does one know where the journey of honesty begins? How can one embark on such a journey when all they know are the lies presented to them, disguised as the truth? How can one advocate to the other such a concept that is so sought, yet is forever misunderstood by a confused and misguided population?

Of all things desired amongst humanity, honesty is the most coveted but hardest to find. Each day, this concept evades the billions who live in a world filled with nothing but the ideas and perspectives found throughout human history. Every day, tons of information, sensory exchanges, and cognitive synapses occur within the individual that hinders them from discerning what is of a subjective nature and what is of an objective nature. With each fleeting moment, the individual moves through a world they never understand. Their interactions come from a survivalist nature, so much so that nothing else is genuine. Nothing is more real to a person than this conclusion. Yet what truly hinders people from truth is the lack of honesty they have about themselves.

The path to truth starts with honesty. The journey of the soul is an attempt to find honesty within oneself. It is an attempt to look beyond the lies. To look beyond the words, phrases, opinions, and perspectives of others, to find one's self. All things begin with honesty. The truth begins with honesty. The search for one's essence begins with honesty. The identity of the individual begins with honesty. Yet who is willing to embark on a journey whose fruits are spiritual rather than material in nature? The downfall of most individuals is their desire to seek refinement and sophistication outwardly while disregarding their inward nature. Ironically, this idea is contradictory in the sense that the more refined a human creation is outwardly, the more it would appear that they are refined inwardly as well. Yet the more advanced and sophisticated human beings become on the outside, the more they lose those qualities on the inside. This comes at a price. To be better than what we are, we create that which is better than us in the ways we feel that we lack. We give it form. We make it tangible. We give it something that is physical so that we may see the perfections we lack and be reminded that we are greater than what we think we are. Yet when such perfections fade, what are we left with? Why create a physical vessel better than us, yet fail to realize that with time, it will fade as we fade?

Honesty. For as long as we live, we may never be privy to it, for it is a fleeting thing. Yet it will be here long after our time; we just won't be there to see it. It is something that only the individual can seek. It is a part of the soul that we deny ourselves to conform and find common ground with other. But in the end, we will never be satisfied. For such a truth sought with others will only be skewed by their various perspectives as well as the human need to be right above all things. Honesty is something sought by all individuals. Although honesty is an expansive concept, it is too narrow for the minds of youth governed by their imagination, not their heart. It is a part of the soul that chooses to look past the illusions we succumb to in order to cope with the world around us. It is something that is the key to our liberation. It is the antidote to our pain, our misery, our suffering. It is the key to overcoming our delusional psyches about the truth of who we are and what we face as human beings.

In accordance with it, we become so much more. More than our baser instincts, more than our lower selves. With it, we may find not only virtue and peace, but our true selves. With it, that which was denied to us can be within our grasp. It is found within the soul. It is first encountered by the ability to question that which bothers us, plagues us, and stands out to us. It starts with a doubt in one's mind, followed by the willingness, not the intellect, to seek that which others believe is unworthy of their attention. Only those who seek to find their own way will discover it. Only those who refuse to believe what lies in front of them will seek it. Only those who are willing to let go of what was once professed to them as truth will find the answer for themselves. When you think you have it, it will not be there. When you think you found it, you will fall short. Trying to force such a thing only leads to your own ignorance. Trying to obtain it like you would power will only consume you until there is nothing left.

Honesty only comes when one admits that they know nothing, when one has reached their lowest point and is willing to accept life as it is, not how they want it to be. It only comes to those who are willing to let go of what they believe to be true and are willing to accept what is true. For when one begins to recognize that honesty is a force they cannot control, cannot manipulate, only then will they begin to understand. They will begin to understand that what they always sought, they always had. They will begin to understand that when one adopts the principles of honesty, all that once confused them will be made clear. When one walks in honesty, peace is possible. When one walks in honesty, they cannot deny what is truth. For when one walks in honesty, they walk in clarity. When one walks in honesty, they walk in principles, in the pursuit of becoming their higher being. When one walks in honesty, they do not settle for what they once were, nor what others believe.

Honesty, it speaks to an individual who is willing to be more than their lower form and their baser instincts. Honesty, it speaks to a part of human nature that is willing to seek the truth in a world of lies. Honesty, it speaks to a virtue that few are willing to seek to gain a higher, more refined human nature. Honesty, it speaks to the individual who knows nothing and accepts that truth. For it is an acceptance in which an individual understands that they are not more than what they are but are willing to be better because of it. Honesty, it speaks to the individual who is willing to take a journey of self to face who they truly are. It speaks to the person who is ready to face reality, to come to terms with their own character, faults, flaws, shortcomings, weaknesses, ambitions, goals, desires, fantasies, self-crafted illusions. It speaks to the individual who is willing to find out for themselves what they could not discover from others. Honesty, it speaks to the part of the human soul that seeks truth above all things. It speaks to the part of the human soul that is willing to find objectivity in a world riddled with subjectivity. It speaks to the person who seeks wisdom and values its fruits above all else. It speaks to something the human soul longs for, but is denied. Honesty, it speaks to the individual who seeks that which is higher than themselves, greater than themselves, despite the reality that they live in the realm of the physical form one that is forever changing. It speaks to a never-ending journey. A journey to be truthful, upright, and honest with oneself. With every encounter, it speaks to the nature of the individual that they knew or never knew existed. they realize they will always fall short because of their inability to be better than the lies others tell them and the ones they tell themselves. As a result, they realize they are weak and because they are weak, they refuse to be anything else. They begin to realize that they lack the strength to overcome the lies they tell themselves and others, and because of it, will continue to live with the delusions and fantasies of their own psyches.

Honesty is the path to truth, and truth the path to Freedom.

CHAPTER 15

INDEPENDENCE

ndependence. Since the dawn of mankind, there has always been a uniqueness to it. It is more than just the physical form, more than just the intellectual capacity. One cannot see it by looking solely at one's outward appearance, for such distinction goes deeper than that. The uniqueness that separates each person lies within their spirit. It is their spirit that shapes their perspective. And it is their difference in perspective that leads to their own independence. Such a concept eluded man at first, since he was not of the sound mind he is today. Many years ago, man believed all things were one and the same, including himself. Yet with time, others among him began to think for themselves as they grew sophisticated in nature. With time, the oneness he had due to his ignorance lead him to drift apart from those he knew. With time, everyone came to have their own perspective and came into their own mind. Some sought to understand forces greater than themselves, others chose to worship of their own accord that which was greater than them, and still others chose to live lives forged by their own hands. With time, one's uniqueness became the source of their independence, the belief that an individual can be who they have always been within.

Independence is the belief that all people are created to forge their own path. Many believe that all were created equally. Each will go on to use such freedom to become their own individual. With such a belief came different perspectives. With different perspectives came conflict. And with conflict, came war. Wars were fought in the name of such an ideal. Independence went from a battle of ideals to a battle of perspectives. It is the fight to come to one's own conclusion. It is the fight to prove that one is right and the other is wrong. It is the understanding of something in a way only an individual or a group of like-minded people can. In a way, independence separates each living thing from the other. It is further enhanced by the difference in one's physical form and outward appearance. Each of us strives for their own individuality as well as the willingness to grow into their uniqueness. Independence is the yearning of the individual to become their own person. It is the yearning of the person to become that which they can call their own. As one seeks that which they claim to form their own person, they further yearn to bask in their own uniqueness. For such uniqueness is something that is sacred to the individual. It speaks to them in ways that only they can understand. For it is the source by which they move. It is the very reason that they draw breath. It is the very thing that gives them passion. To the individual, it is the uniqueness that is a part of them that gives purpose to all they do in life. It fuels their being. It guides them to a path that they must one day walk on their own. It brings them to a place in their heart where they must ask themselves, "what do I want to live for"? what is worth living for? What is worth living for while I draw breath"? What is the one thing I want to commit to that will give my life meaning and my actions purpose? It is a desire of the human soul to express that which is inward. For the person one becomes a the reflection of their soul.

Self-expression, It speaks to the yearning of a person to express who they have always been within. It speaks of a desire that all people have, yet many ignore. It speaks to a spiritual yearning denied by the demands of the material world and the desires of one's flesh. Yet many do not know who they are. The illusions of oneself as they present themselves to others convolutes their idea of who they really are. For self-expression is that of the soul. It is something everyone can possess but express differently. Some seek it in the form of physical movements. It is the expenditure of energy, to turn their weak physical frame into a marvel that all can relish. It is the goal for the individual to surpass their innate physical limitations. They seek constant repetition to the point where such mundane movements become sophisticated bodily instincts grounded in principles of physical refinement. These individuals are, driven to be more than their primitive instincts their corporeal being. Self-expression is to take all that passion, all that energy that comes from their animalistic nature and turn it into something more than that of the beast of the fields. For them, it is to turn a beast into a man.

Some seek self-expression by way of the mind. Some seek a higher intellect and a deeper understanding as their form of self-expression. To them, higher thought, critical thinking, philosophical insights of the highest order are their benchmark of a sophisticated being. It is the pursuit of knowledge, the understanding of the mysterious, the oneness with the essence of that which is unknown where such beings seek self-expression. There are those who seek the outward, the lavish, the exquisite, the flamboyant. To these individuals, it is by way of the materialistic that they display to others and themselves who they are. This culminates in fashion, styles, individualistic expressions of one's character and personality. Weird to the on looker, these individuals believe that who they are cannot be contained by way of the traditional norms set forth by those of old. Then there are those of the spiritual nature. They seek self-expression through a way of life. They, embrace that which is of a standard, a moral, a principle, a guiding force in their life that, will help them overcome any situation and be better because of it. For these individuals, it is not by fancy words or lavish praise from others that they seek to express their inner being, but by way of the path they walk. They cannot put into words the full meaning of what it is they seek; the only way to understand their destination is to embark on the same journey. For them, self-expression has no words, only actions. For them, self-expression has no material rewards but is a lifelong test of the code they live by. It does not concern physical, social, political, or mental matters. Instead it is of a spiritual matter. It is the daily test to determine if they can be more than what they believe themselves to be. To them, it is something more than what others can understand. For them, it is a lonely path that cannot be explained to those who do not seek it as they do. To them, it is something more, something that even they cannot explain to themselves, yet endure in their quest for self- knowledge. With time, deeper mysteries, a deeper understanding of themselves becomes clear. And with time, peace becomes apparent.

How is a boy able to become a man? How is a girl ever to become a woman? How is a child able to grow into the adult it will one day become? How is a student ever to become the master? How is the outcast who views what others do differently ever to become the genius that may better humanity? How is the potential, the greatness, the power that lurks within an individual ever to grow and manifest itself if they are hindered by the expectations of the dominant ideas and principles? How does every person come to the same understanding if they are unique in their own way?

Independence is a funny thing. It is the right of all beings; the problem with it lies the direction it will lead humanity in the years to come. For an abundance of perspectives does not amount to anything if it leads the masses to their doom. Each person will have their own ideas, their subjective biases, their own sense of right and wrong, and their own way of life. But which is right? Which will lead humanity down a greater path? Which will bring people together rather than tear them apart? Which will lead society to a greater understanding than the one is that came before it? How many more wars will be fought because of it? How many will die to defend their own unique perspective? How many will be sacrificed in the pursuit of their own form of self-expression?

The problem of independence lies with the individual. Often, each person chooses to express who they are, yet they do not know who they are. They try as many outlets as they can to find what suits them the most, going through so much only to find so little. Many fall slave to the perspectives of others and become someone else rather than their own being. Some become so captivated by what they see that who they are depends on their senses rather than their own reflective nature. Many misunderstand independence. Their interpretation allows them to behave recklessly believing they can do whatever they want whenever they want. Others understand independence as a license to express their views in spite of the opinions of others. Although they attempt to communicate their own individuality, they do not know who they are. They do not know if what they do reflects their soul or is merely a way to comply with a demand required to survive in the world. But the question to ask is how is independence to be expressed? How does one express their inner being without offending another? How does one become who they are without hindering the growth of others? How does one express who they are while being a light to others? If humanity has the luxury to be more than its baser instincts, if each individual is fortunate enough to be different from those among them, what is the best means of being and expressing who they are?

Independence, it speaks to the one thing that will determine who we will become. For the yearnings of every heart are different as they speak to that which governs the soul. Everyone possesses a gift specific to them. Some possess a heart big enough to care when others do not. Some possess the ability to understand lives they have not lived. Some possess a mind that will one day be a gift to mankind. Some possess the strength necessary to take a stand for what is right when others have lost their will to fight. Many will grow to become all they believe to be the epitome of their individuality. Many will fulfill what they truly believe is their calling. Yet none shall stand the same. Many will grow to be advocates, leaders, thinkers, inventors, innovators, healers of the body, seers of the soul. Everyone will grow to become what they believe to be true and just. What each soul becomes offers insight into the duality yet diversity of the human experience. In a way, independence is proof that one can become their own individual and forge their own path. It is proof that everyone can be the example they seek to be. For each heart is unique in what it can offer to the world.

As we look back, Independence has been a source of humanity's greatest triumphs. It has allowed people to strive for what they believe to be the change that will liberate the blind and free themselves from that which hinders the world. It has led to the creation of the tools, inventions, philosophies, technologies, advancements, sophistications, and ways of life that has allowed humanity to see better days than the ones of old. However, it was also independence that led others to the development of a unique perspective that was the incarnation of death. It has led to wars grounded in ignorance yet fought for greed. It has led to the death of millions in the name of a faith that was never their own. It has led to the scars that still plague modern man today. This uniqueness of perspective still holds humanity back from seeking the idea of oneness and unity that it strives to achieve. Like all force's unseen to the naked eye, it is an influence one cannot control, manipulate, or, cannot thoroughly breakdown. The only way it can be understood is by way of a spiritual journey. Independence, like all things, is something the individual must come to understand for themselves. With time, such an understanding can do more good than harm. But lacking such an understanding can lead an individual to become a shadow of what they could have been, a regression of the epitome of their true potential.

Independence, it is a funny thing. But with time, patience, and understanding, it can be a gift to mankind.

CHAPTER 16

HOPE

iving in this world, you do not know what good is. Living in this world, you do not know what faith is. Living in this world, you do not know what hope is. Living in this world, you do not know what to fight for, what to long for that will enrich your soul. Living in this world, you do not know what to genuinely believe in as anything and everything can be right and wrong depending on one's point of view. Living in this world, you do not know what good your actions can do. You do not know what good you can bring to the hearts of others, your loved ones, your friends, your family. Living in this world, you do not know what is worthwhile. You do not know what is worth living for, dying for, committing one's life to. Eventually you reach a point where you do not what is worth having hope for. You reach a point where you cannot see what good will come out of what you do. You cannot see the good that lies within people. You cannot see the good that lies within you. And you cannot see the good that can exist in this world. You ask yourself is there anything left in this world that has not been corrupted by our touch. You ask yourself is there anything left that has not been corrupted by human thought, arrogance, ignorance, greed, gluttony, wrath, fury.

Hope. As you live and look at your life and the world, it gets harder and harder to find. You desperately try to find it, something to believe in, something to fight for, something that is pure in this tainted world. As you think, you cannot see it. As you breath, you cannot feel it. And as you live, you just cannot believe it. As time goes on, people give you more reasons to not have it than to believe in it. It is almost a myth. It is almost a legend. As you live in this world, you do not know what it is because you do not know where it is found. More so, you do not know if you can have enough of it to put it in something and live by it.

Have you ever felt it, hope? This feeling that there is more than what we see? This feeling that we can be more than what we know? This feeling that there is more to life, more to living than what we think there should be? The more sophisticated people become and the better they can put into words what something is, the more they reduce it to something that is replicable, expendable, and basic. With so many minds and hearts viewing most, if not all, that they do in this way, it is hard to have hope in anything. It is as if our own attempt to understand the things that do not make sense hinders us when we finally have a concrete grasp of its meaning and implications. It is as if the more we live, the harder it is to have hope in something that others do not see as worth having. Have you ever felt it, hope? Have you ever felt that despite how messed up life is, people are, you are, there is something more? Something better? Have you felt that one's own rational nature and pragmatic approach to everything they do hindered them from having hope in what could be? Have you felt it, this thing called hope? This idea that despite what is, there is a promise of what could be? Something more, something greater, something better? Better than us? Better than what we see? Better than what we know? Better than what we create? Something worth fighting for. Something worth living for. Something worth dying for.

As children, we are led to believe that anything is possible if we believe it. As children, we are told to dream big and become lost in our imaginations. We are told to live in our imaginations and by our childish nature. We are told to dream bigger than what we can imagine. Our parents tell us this because they want us to be better than them. They want us to dream, to hope, and to be the change they wish they could have been. They want us to be idealistic and caring. Deep down, they wish they could have that childish naivete, that ability to forget how things are and see them as they could be. At times, they wish they could let go of their rationality and practicality and just be a kid once more, basking in the infinite space of the childish imagination. Yet as we grow older, we must sacrifice that which makes us idealistic, that which gave us hope for a brighter tomorrow, that which allowed us to go where those before us never could just to conform to the ways of the world. In that moment, we die. We stop believing in the good that can come about if we dream if we believe. We stop thinking that somewhere in our hearts lies something that separates us from others. In that moment, we have nothing left to dream for, nothing to believe in. In that moment, we lose that part of us that made living worthwhile. We lose that part that never knew how to give up. We lose that part of us that would fight on and believe.

At this point, it becomes hard to be the change you want to see. It becomes hard to believe that one person can make a difference for the greater good. It gets harder to think that there is any good left in humanity. It gets hard to live, hard to breath, hard to commit yourself to a life where you want to be that change. At that point, it gets hard for one to be the example they believed they could be. Living, but not seeing the change you thought you would see; it becomes that much harder to be what you believe in. It gets hard to have hope. It gets hard to have faith. It gets hard to walk down the path that you believe is true, is just, is right, and that means everything to you. It gets hard to be the beacon of light in a world where all people know is darkness. It gets hard to take a stand in what you believe in and fight for it with all your resolve, with all your being. It gets harder to be idealistic and live by such a philosophy. In that moment, it gets hard to walk the journey because the journey itself will put you at odds with all those you meet. You do not know how much you must or can give, when you think you have nothing left. You never know if all that you do is enough to satisfy yourself, let alone help others to see what you believe. In your heart, you are always uneasy as you do not know what it is you are looking for. Yet you are guided by the hunch that you believe that somewhere it, is out there. You tell yourself that if you have hope, it will be enough. But the more you live and breathe, the more you think to yourself that it's not there, the more the journey become less worthwhile. The only thing you come to understand is that the world and the people who live in it will always give you more reasons to doubt hope, to give up on it than to put your faith in it.

You continue to fight because you believe in your heart there is something more, something you do not see, but feel. You cannot describe it to others because it is something that one must experience for themselves; it cannot be found in an academic text. It is something that can only be understood in the soul, not by the mind. It is this thing called hope. Although it has many names for example, courage, will, and takes many forms, it is all the same.

What is hope? The standard definition of hope is a feeling of expectation and a desire for a certain thing to happen. But is that it? Is there more to it than that? Is hope this feeling you know in your heart, in your soul that one can be more, one can achieve more, that things can be different? Is that hope or is that idealism? At times, the two are so entangled, so interchangeable that it is hard to understand which is which. What is hope and how does one know if it truly exists? What is hope and how does one acquire it? There is a difference between studying something and experiencing it. You can never capture the essence of what something is and give it a physical form or verbal definition / description and expect others to have the same understanding.

So, what does it mean to have hope? What does it mean to put your hope in others? Is it a fool's errand? Is it grounded in the belief that people can be more than what they are, even if they do not see it themselves? Is it grounded in the belief that there is something worth fighting for in this world? Something that will change people and mankind for the greater good? Is it grounded in the belief that this idea of unity, human excellence, individual merit, equality is possible despite our differences? Does hope speak to the fact that there is more to people than the physical body, the logical and reasoning capabilities we have? Does it speak to the idea that what lies within the human soul, that which is dormant in each individual, that uniqueness, that individuality that each person possesses, can one day be the thing that draws us closer to the utopia that our ancestors thought could come to pass? Does hope to speak to what people can become, united on a common front? Does it speak to the idea that despite our differences, we can come together and be more? More than what history has remembered us by: slavery, war, genocide, hatred, imperialism, misguided nationalism? Does hope speak to the idea that what was impossible is possible if we believe it and work toward it, no matter how childish, how idealistic, how foolish it may sound? Does hope speak to that spark, that ember that burns within us to be the change that so many before us have fought for and failed at? Does it speak to the idea that humanity was wrong about its greatest gift ,the mind, and that there is something more, something dormant inside all of us? Could this thing be the soul, which allows us to be more than our baser instinct, our primitive nature, and instead be what those before us knew we could be (better than them)?

Is it wrong to have hope? Is it wrong to believe that despite what one believes that something good can come out of it? Is it wrong to be hopeful despite what one will, and must, endure? Is it wrong to fight the good fight? Is it wrong to be hopeful despite the atrocities of the past, and stand for what one believes to be right, to be true, to be just? Is it wrong to have hope when one is so engulfed by darkness they cannot even fathom being in the presence of the light? Is it wrong to have hope in what could be rather than what is? But what if what you hope for is not irrational? Does that make you right or wrong? Does that make your ideology correct? Does it make your actions taken vain and unjustifiable?

What must one endure to rely on hope rather than intellect? How miserable, how let down, how spiritually torn must a person be to understand what it means to have hope? Does such torment come from seeing the world as it is and, being conflicted as to how it should be? Where others rely on data, statistics, empirical evidence, and scientific methods, the one who has hope relies on their emotions, their heart, what they believe to be true. Is hope a sign of weakness in the sense that those who rely on it lack the capability to get anything done by their own merit? Does it make a person weak in the sense that they rely on an ideal and do not accept the pragmatic perspective that the masses rely on? Does having more hope in what you believe than what you can produce lead to being at odds with the world? Is hope for the peasant? Is it for those who only know suffering? Is it for those who rely on higher power rather than forging their own path? Is hope for the mistreated? Is it for the slave, the subservient? Is it for those who know only negativity? Is hope the idea that one can expect great things to happen in a world they view as negative and unchangeable?

Is hope for the weak?

Is hope a sign of weakness?

When one looks at people, at all that we are, at all that we create, at all that elevates us, and focuses on the things that lead to their down fall, is there hope for us? When one looks at the history of humans and their arrogance, ignorance, shortcomings, and strengths, is there hope for us? When one looks at the individuals who have gone on to define an era, a point in time, and were remembered throughout history for what they stood for and accomplished, is there hope for us? When one looks at those who paved the way for the next generation who had the world at their very fingertips and pulled the strings, is there hope for us? When one thinks about all the wrong that was done by those who adopted a faith, that was never theirs, and committed horrific acts in the name of that faith, is there hope for us? In man's ignorance and perpetual lack of understanding of what he truly possesses the power to shape the future, is there hope for us? In humanity's attempt to be more than what it is by discovering the truth behind its existence, is there hope for us?

As people come into their own, is there hope for them? As each generation goes on to achieve what those before them never could, is there hope for it? As new generations confront forces and pursue advancements unknown to them, is there hope for them? As people fight amongst themselves over-power, fame, prestige, the need to be right, and their self-fulfilling prophecy, is there hope for them? As wars are fought to protect and secure one man's greed, one nations perspective, is there hope for us? As civil disputes wage on, as people grapple with the philosophical truth of whether co-existence is possible and not a dream, is there hope for us? As science continues to leap forward at a rate faster than the mind can grasp, is there hope for us? As humanity steps into a new age, one that came faster than those of our ancient ancestors, are we ready to face what our untold future will bring? As nations wield more power than we thought possible, is there hope that we can learn to universally control, and master this strength to build a better tomorrow? As we become more pragmatic, more intelligent, less reliant on faith and religion, and more reliant on rational thought and logic, is there hope for us? As we become more practical and less moral, is there hope for us? As we focus on what we can outwardly produce rather than bask in who we spiritually are, is there hope for us? As we steer away from the traditions of the old and come into our own, is there hope for us? As we grow into our individuality as part of our generation, how will history remember us? How will those who live on remember us when we die? Will they come to judge us as those who had the hope to build a world that was better than the one, they know? Or will they see us as failures who did not bring about change?

Why should one have hope?

Is there hope for us as we enter the new era?

When I look at this world, I am forever reminded of how different I am. Each day reminds me of who I am, and how well I meet the demands imposed on others and the governing philosophies of the world. Every day is a test. A test of will, a test of skill, a test of intelligence, but also test of heart. I have come to learn that people are universally both pragmatic and impulsive. No other cognitive function governs them than these two. In times of crisis, and in times of victory, they are pragmatic as well as impulsive. People know how to flock together when they are of one accord, and many times they do so by being logical. It is this mindset that allows them to come to a common consensus, yet it is this mindset that hinders them from finding a solution to a problem that is greater than themselves.

As I have come to walk the earth, I have come to understand that only the Individual can hope. The group can only agree on what can be done by way of action, but it is only the Individual that can hope for what they believe in. With a group comes an institution. An institution of ideas. An institution governed by its own philosophies. But like all institutions, groups fall victim to bureaucracy, and therefore, they fall.. While there is strength in numbers, there is always a lack of understanding. After a while, the group believes an institutional idea, not a personal belief that each has come to accept for themselves. The loneliness that comes with this realization makes the journey that much harder. For as long as one pursues the idea of hope, what it can mean for themselves and, others, and how it can shape the world, they will forever be alone. Their belief in such an idealistic endeavor will be the worst battle they must face. They live in a world that gives them more reasons to hate the world and what people do than to see what they can accomplish if they work towards it. They will look at this world, see the basic nature of man, and conclude that in the end, that is all he is capable of. They will look at the history, the methods, the ideologies, the thinking of various institutions created by man and come to understand that despite all that people are capable of, this is the best they can produce. They will wonder why those who ask for freedom are the same individuals who suffer the way they do because they abuse the very thing they ask for. People with hope will never understand how others can settle for something less, fail to realize their potential, yet ask of the next generation more than what came before it. And in that moment, they must ask themselves if despite all this, they still want to have hope in something others will never believe in. Sometimes; it must be someone willing to become better because of their beliefs who must have the faith to be more than the world has led them to think they could. It is when we weather the storm that we will get the opportunity to become better because we are willing to do so. And it is when we choose to have hope and commit all that we do to such an ideal that we grow closer to building a world that is truly worth living for.

That is why, one must have hope.

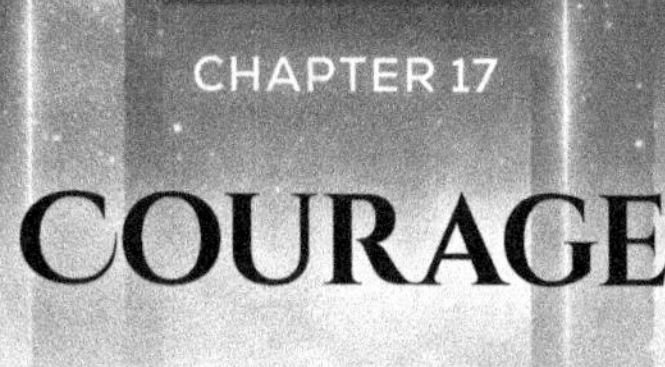

COURAGE

Within the human soul is the capacity to overcome that which afflicts us. Within us as human beings is something that allows us to have what it takes to venture into the unknown or that which frightens us. Within us is the capability to overcome fear and become who we were meant to be. When the mind tells us no, when those around us do not have the answers we seek, when we are afraid to walk a path the direction of which is unknown, something within us allows us to venture there for ourselves. Something within us allows us to push past the things that hold us back. Where logic tells us no, faith is what allows us to see what can be. Where fear hinders us from walking the path others are not willing to take, something else allows us to walk down the path and grow closer to achieving our goal.

To describe what courage is in words does not do it justice. For what I speak of must be felt, must be lived, must be experienced by the individual. So many claims to walk their own path but, fall short of what they could become. Many claim that they possess all that is needed for the journey ahead, yet they speak only to the physical and mental attributes. Yet what I speak of is the spirit. Many claim that they walk their own path, yet they are too afraid to be their own individual. Many are so logical that they do not know what it means to walk by faith or endure when logic will not suffice. Many believe that what they possess is more than enough to see them through any situation, yet what they believe they possess, they lack. Many claim that only the mind and body are necessary to achieve what it is they seek, yet they do not understand. In the modern era, logic and pragmatism is all they know. Yet there is more to being human than what one can perceive, or what one knows. Many see the fundamentals of victory as possessing skills, qualities, attributes, and traits that make anything possible. Many believe that by knowing these, that they possess them. While they are not wrong in such regard, it is more than knowing what to possess,. Such things must be lived, pondered, and experienced, and can only be known by self-reflection and honesty of self. Many will not understand what it takes.

To modern-day generations, everything is academic in nature. And because of that, they do not know what it means to feel, to understand. For such things must be lived, not studied. Many claim they possess what is necessary to make a difference in this world. Many claim they possess what is necessary to endure when all they know will fail them. Many claim they possess what is necessary to be an example for those who come along after they pass. But do they? Such a boast is made by those of little experience. To make such a claim speaks to their level of understanding. For what do they possess that will make a difference to themselves and those around them? What must one possess to be the change they seek to be? What is it that will make one stand out from others? What is it that will make one fight for what they believe, and be willing to endure when all they know has failed them? COURAGE.

Courage, the quality of the admirable. It speaks to one who seeks to overcome fear, venture into the unknown, and stand up for what they believe to be true and just, even if others do not. It speaks to something that one must experience. For true courage cannot be put into words, but is shown by action. Of all the qualities, attributes, character traits, and principles sought by man, courage is the one that makes one stand out the most. We admire those who show great courage because it reminds us that where fear can trap us, courage can free us. They tell us that by way of courage, we can overcome our greatest fears.

Courage, it speaks to the proud, the strong, the bold, the fearless. It speaks to those who will go where none have gone before. It speaks to those willing to do what others will not. For those who seek courage do not desire it for the perceptions it will give us in the eyes of others. They seek what will push them to a place where logic will not be useful, where faith and the comfort of those close to them will not be enough. Like all things known to man, on the surface, the definition of courage is clear, but when embodied on the spiritual level it is more complex. For the fault of all people is believing that they understand all that they know. Courage is something that no group will ever understand. Courage itself and the pursuit to know what it means is a journey of its own. To overcome their insecurities, many, if not all, people say that they know what courage is and what it means. Many say they possess it, yet many are aloof to what it really is.

All people believe courage is something easy to possess because they have not felt the need for it. If they were thrust into a position where the result was uncertain and their life hung in the balance, would they have the courage necessary to overcome or to endure the situation? Their understanding of it is academic, and their application of it is minimal. To put courage into words would be a fallacy, for reason cannot explain what is found within the heart. It is my belief that only the individual can possess courage. Groups will wither, fade, fall short of their own agendas, and become corrupt by the one thing they first sought in their pursuit. For courage is pursued not for its name sake, but when an individual has reached the end of all reason. It is sought when they logically doubts what they believe in, what they believe to be true, and what they fight for. Yet within them is the spark of hope, an ember of faith. On the one hand, they doubt what they believe in. On the other, in their heart they hold fast to their beliefs. And at some point, they come to the understanding that if they are to continue down the path they are on, where they will not know what to expect, but are willing to endure what will follow, they must have courage to see their journey it through to the end.

———

What is courage? Many know of its definition, but what of its visceral meaning? What does it mean to possess courage?

What is courage? Is it a feeling, and emotion? Is it found in the human mind? Is it found within the human soul? Is it found within the human body? Is it just an attribute that describes the bold, sometimes erratic behavior of the hero? Something that lets one act when all their natural impulses and survival instincts tells them not to? Is courage something one is born with? Is it something that anyone can possess? Is it a skill, a quality, a trait, a gift? Does it reflect the nature, the essence of the soul who embodies it? Is it something that you can learn? Is it something that you can hone? If courage is something of the heart, why do so many believe they possess it when they are not in tune with their spiritual, inward nature? If courage is something housed within the body, why does it not show within our genetic makeup? If someone describes what courage is and what it meant to possess it, do they know what it means to have it, and do they possess it themselves? What is courage? Is it a desire of the spirit to overcome fear? Is it the ability of an individual to forge their own path, be their own individual, even though they are unsure of what lies ahead? Is it the ability to endure when all that we know, all that we knew, and all that we came to terms with fails? Is courage the answer as to how one shapes the future? How one fights the good fight? How one overcomes oppression? Is it acknowledging what few do, let alone face by themselves? Is it something that will remain in the eyes of certain death? Is it something that allows you to fight the good fight, even when those you thought would stand amongst you are gone? Is courage something that human beings got right? Do we have the right definition, the right understanding of the word? Is courage something that all people will ever come to accept and possess to the same degree?

Will we ever know what it truly means to have courage?

The shame of each generation is that they boast about something they will never truly possess. Each brags as they claim they are better than the ones who came before them. They claim that the reason they are able to achieve what the others did not is that they possess what the other never knew or never had. The downfall of each person is believing that what others can achieve, they can achieve. No two people are the same, nor will they accomplish the same things. It is not that they are willing, not capable, not intelligent, not worthy, not skillful. Some have little to no courage; others, just enough; and still others, more than anyone will ever know. It is this difference that separates those who are remembered by history who acted despite what others believed, from those who listened to what was accepted as universal truth. It is this difference that separates one who let fear grip them and controls all that they do from those willing to venture out and find what lies more beyond the horizon. It is courage that separates the proud, the cocky, the arrogant, the ignorant from the willing, the faithful. It is courage that separates those who follow facts, statistics, and the pragmatic understandings of the masses from those guided by idealistic dreams of the heart, dreams that make them foolish enough to fight for their beliefs. It is the understanding of what courage is and what it means that will separate the actions and deeds done by each person. It will determine what they are capable of and what they believe to be worth living for and worth dying for. It is this understanding and the possession of courage that allows someone to change the world by taking a path they believe to be true, defying public opinion.

Our beliefs about courage may be true in keeping with our subjective opinion. But it is our actions that will govern whether we truly have what it takes to go down that path in search of who we truly are. For courage is not for the weak to be strong, but for the weak to be stronger. For courage is not a badge of honor to be paraded and celebrated by the masses. Nor is it something to be crowned like royalty. For courage is not something tangible, nor can it be shown to people by way of some materialistic means. It cannot be housed within a single entity, but only embodied in one's heart. Where logic fails us, and faith may not be enough, it is through courage where we may come to find what we seek to be true in our own heart's. For courage is something that is not awarded from one to another; it is something that must be pondered, experienced, endured, pondered, and fought for, if one is to understand what it means to truly possess it.

For true courage is not spoken but displayed through action.

Why should we possess courage?

There will come a day where each person must stand tall and be honest with themselves. There will come a day when everyone must face an existential battle with themselves. One day, each person must ask themselves who they are, what they want, and whether they are willing to become the person they always knew they could be. Someday, they must stop running, stop hiding from who they are and what they possess. They must come to understand that what they truly possess can never be put into words, only spoken through action. And they must come to understand that since they cannot describe to others in full detail or make others come to the same understanding of what they possess, they must be willing to venture on their own, journey to become their own individual. Despite the loneliness they will feel, the uneasiness of such a journey, and the ambiguity of such a path, they must have courage when all else fails them. They must come to have courage when all they know, all they knew, all they thought was true has failed them. Even when they think that all they knew was a lie, they must possess courage. When they believe their hopes and dreams too idealistic for a pragmatic world, they must have courage. Sometimes, in fact, all the time, it is an idealistic heart and mind that shapes and changes the world when others are too pragmatic and logical to see what the true solution is. Sometimes, it is the heart that is willing, not the mind that is pragmatic, to make the changes needed to make the world a better place. There will come a day where each person, no matter their persona, social status and prestige, wealth, access to goods and resources must ask if they possess what is necessary to be who they believe they were always meant to be. There will come a day when each person will find out if they possess the level of courage they boast. One day, a time will come where their words will need to be backed up by the actions, which will represent what they believe to be true. It is that moment that will speak to their character, to their beliefs, to their nature more than any words they have ever uttered. When faced by a threatening situation, they do not know if they will be gripped by fear, doubt, or anxiety. They will not know what got ahold of them. For they must dig deep, get to a place where their logical point of view is inadequate. It will be the only thing that guides them when everything else fails. It will be the only thing they can call on when all they thought to be true has left them, and are forever at odds with a world that will never understand them. It will be the only thing that allows them to continue to walk down the path they doubt but believe to be true.

What they must possess, if they are willing, is courage.

CHAPTER 18

FORGIVENESS

iving in this world, people do not know how to forgive. We may not even know what it means. The wrongs of others always linger with us in a way that hurts the most. They vex us, plagues us, annoys us, toy with us, claw at us, an irritating feeling you cannot shake. No matter where we go, those who have wronged us, hurt us in ways that cut deep, always seem to be with us. No matter where we run, the hurt is always there. It is there in our actions, our choices, our decision making, how we treat others. Some speculate that the reason we do not know what forgiveness is or what it means is because it is not part of us. Some think that forgiveness is yet another concept created by a mind trying to make sense of a feeling or a sensation unknown to the human entity. Some say that forgiveness is a principle created to help create the ideal human being. Some believe that while it may not lie within us, it can be adopted and used to guide us mere mortals down the path to becoming a better human being.

As I walk the earth, I see that people truly are of a base nature. They are prone to impulse, instinct, and desires of the flesh, ignoring principles or anything that relates to being of an "ideal "nature. But when it comes to forgiveness, they struggle as we all do. They treat the idea loosely in the sense that they claim to have possession of something they do not know. They claim to have knowledge of something that they do not understand. Thus, their interpretation and implementation of forgiveness is poor. Maybe it is their nature, maybe it is their psyche, who knows? Even in religion, the gods or the entities they believe to be their creator show some level of forgiveness, yet they cannot show it amongst themselves.

I have come to find that many would trade forgiveness for revenge since it would bring them immediate comfort. It is in that comfort that they find satisfaction, yet they are never at peace. I have come to see that many neglect forgiveness because they see it as something born from a weak nature. They see forgiveness as not dealing with an issue head on, or letting off the hook the person who is the source of their suffering. It is because of the instant sense of satisfaction that many people value revenge, retribution, the eye-for-an-eye approach over forgiveness. Yet some do not know what it means to forgive. Some cannot fathom letting go of the wrongs done to them by someone else, allowing that person to live and not feel the same as they did. Some people do not understand how to move on and let the deeds of the past remain in the past. For some people, living in anger and, bitterness, and holding a grudge gives them purpose or a sense of meaning that nothing else could. Some people express these feelings in vengeance, in violence, in rage, in having hatred for others. As I have walked this earth, I have come to understand that so many cannot forgive because they do not know how to forgive. So many cannot forgive because they do not know what it means to have forgiveness in their heart's. And some people cannot forgive because they do not know how to live with it.

Have you ever known forgiveness? If you could, how would you describe it? Could you put it into words? Could you express it in action? But could you say you truly possess it? At what point did you know for sure if you did? Did you know that it was abundant in you? Could you feel it? Could you sense it? Could you perceive it? Could you understand it? If you could, how would you give it form? How would you give it breadth? How would you give it meaning? How would you give it purpose? How could you universalize for all what you believe to be true? Have you ever felt the burden of huer you've carried leave you when you accept what the other did and learn to move on? Have you ever felt the weight leave your psyche? Have you ever learned to let go of the anger, the bitterness, the wrath you have had towards another? If so, how? How does one possess what they do not have? Have does one express what they never thought possible? How does one accept what is not universally acceptable? We obtain forgiveness by expressing it to others. But if it is not understood or articulated by all in the same manner, how can we say that what we believe is forgiveness, is accurate?

We never forget those who have wronged us, who hurt us, who let us down. We never forget how much pain they caused when they stuck the knife in us where it hurt most. We never forget the intent behind it, the surprise it brought us, because we never saw it coming and we let our guard down. We never forget the forms of justification used to excuse such acts by those who caused them. Such wounds, such desires, such passions, such things can transcend lifetimes. They can hinder generations to come. They can spark war and hinder peace. Such things can be the divider of nations, of cultures, of ideas, of ways of thinking, of religious sects, between right and wrong. Acts committed out of malice can be the very thing that breaks an individual to the point where they can never recover. Moreover hurt people, hurt others.

How much could have been avoided if one person said they were sorry? How much could have been avoided if one person stepped forth and took responsibility for their actions? How much death could have been prevented if one forgave the other? How much would have been different if one party admitted to the other the error of their ways and both learned to move on and live? How different would history be if the most powerful kingdoms came to more than a truce, learned to forgive the other, and became better for it? How different would life be today if instead of holding dear to the wrongs done by those in the past, those who suffered had, learned to absolve and, let go?

Forgiveness is this tricky thing you cannot quite put your hands on. It is something you do not know if you possess, yet it is something you give to others when you or they understand the fault of your ways.

But why should one forgive?

As you look back, you find that it is not easy to let go of the things of the past. Some groups of people, may never move forward. Others may, live in the present. But, every second they draw breath, they remember how their future was shaped by a past that was never chosen for them, yet always controls them. The circumstances under which some people live are due to events that transpired in the past. Even with the capability to progress forward and achieve what those before thought impossible, the roadblocks of yesterday still influence today. But, when you think about it, should they forgive the deeds that enslave them today? In the most extreme cases, is it easy to wash away the blood, the death, the hatred, the anger, the atrocities, committed by those whose own ignorance and fear of death led to the demise of millions? Is it as simple as saying I forgive you? Is it as simple as turning the other cheek? Is it easy for anyone to forgive? Is forgiveness necessary in every situation? Are compensation and, reparations sometimes required as an act of forgiveness? Or are words enough? Is it easy to move on when your future may be determined by what was committed in the past? Should groups of people be held accountable for the sins of their forefathers? Even as we try to co-exist, is it easy to live with the descendants of those whose decisions led to the death of so many innocents? Is it easy to live in the new age where we will forever deal with the choices, decisions, actions, both good and bad, of those who came before us? Can we find peace without forgiveness? Can we find meaning without it? Can we find purpose without it? If we let go of our hurt, can we experience something more, something greater than what we knew? In forgiving, can we find healing that cannot be found in medicine or any earthly substance used to alleviate or mask pain?

Can we ever learn to forgive others?

Can we ever learn to let the grave deeds of the past go even if they haunt us today?

Can we ever move on knowing that what was done before our time will always hinder us?

Can we ever learn to forgive those who have come before us when they are the one responsible for our suffering?

Why should one have forgiveness?

When you learn to forgive, it is not a sign a weakness, but strength. For many find pride and joy in holding onto the pain that others cause them. Many find peace in holding a grudge against others. But when you live by the sword, you die by the sword. When you live by the pain of the past, you never truly live. You become an outlet for the expression of all the pain and negativity of those who wronged you. To forgive is to move on despite what they project onto you. To forgive means to reject the past and embrace what others have given you. Forgiveness shows the coldhearted something they themselves were never given… love, sympathy, empathy. And sometimes that is all it takes. Yet such a simple thing is something that people do not know how to possess, let alone express. It is easy to let others diminish you the way that they do, but it takes strength to show courtesy, love, sympathy, and empathy towards another who never knew such things existed. For when you forgive, you become the better person. When you forgive, you let the past stay in the past and let the future be determined by what you deem it to be.

Yet forgiveness is not as easy as we think. Somethings are not easy to let go of. Some things hold too much weight, too much pain, too much strife to be forgiven in a single moment. Yet when you learn to forgive, you become the better person. Others will not celebrate you in the way you want them to, but in your heart, you will know. For when you forgive, you feel it. You feel the weight, the bitterness, the pain, the void that could never be filled suddenly vanish. For when you forgive, all that you held inside that ate at you for so long is gone, and, in the end, you are the one who stands victorious. For vengeance is not the way. While the immediate need for action and recompense satisfies us in the moment, in the end, the void remains. And what of those who have also been wronged by others? While forgiveness speaks to being the better person, the road to arrive there is never easy. You will be pressured, pushed, tested in your attempts to find something that others may never come to ever respect. Yet in the end, you will stand tall as others fall to what they cannot let go. You will live and prosper while others sink further into their own abyss. You release the darkness that once consumed you go, while others will never see the light.

Forgiveness speaks to the individual who seeks to be better for it. For the one who seeks forgiveness seeks the path to true healing. And if they are willing, they will find something within them they never knew existed … Life.

CHAPTER 19

ENCOURAGEMENT

As we live life, we do not know what to believe in. As we walk our own paths to what we believe is worth living for, we will never know what is true and what is just. What we do know is that there will be hardship. There will be pain, suffering, malice, and hatred leveled against us by those who do not understand us, that we may not know how to combat. As you look at this world, all you see is the suffering of others at the hands of those who do not care. You see how the faults of others, the misdeeds of others, the apathy of others can lead to the destruction of so many. In this world, evil is more abundant than good. In this world, darkness is more prevalent than light. People try but fail. They try to be better than what they know, than what they are. It is hard to be what you do not know how to be. To be better, to be more, is harder than to be what you innately are. Falling short makes it easier to give up hope, to give up faith, to sacrifice one's dream to fit in. To fight the good fight is no easy feat. But those who fight the hardest for what they believe is worth having never give up. None will understand their battles, their struggle, their pain. None will know how such a journey of self, following beliefs they hold to be true, will conflict them inwardly for as long as they live. Those who suffer in ways not seen to the naked eye do so in ways that go deeper than what others may think. Those who suffer in silence bear what most cannot describe. Internal suffering is more than just a scientific term to describe a bodily and psychological condition. It takes one bad moment to see why there is nothing good in this world, nothing worth living, or fighting, for.

History offers countless examples as to how humanity's nature has often led to its downfall. People's ignorance, fear, arrogance, and limited perspective have many times gotten the better of them and hindered them. How can one come to understand what they truly possess or are capable of if they do not see it for themselves? As you look at this world, you see numerous achievements, advancements, sophistications, discoveries. Yet when you look at human nature, you see that we always fall short. It makes one wonder, are all these accomplishments worth having if we can never learn to be better in our hearts? What good are all these materialistic and scientific achievements if people will never be better in their hearts to truly benefit from them? Why fight for goodness if we are defeated before we even enter battle? If you cannot save people from themselves, then what do you save them from? If people do not know what to fight against, how do they know what to fight for?

Encouragement. No matter how strong we proclaim ourselves to be or, how strong our stature, we will always fail. It is the soul that has fought for so long that does not know how to ask for help. It is the soul that has known nothing but strife and that cannot find comfort in others. It is the soul that has known nothing but hardship that does not know how to receive words of kindness. For such hardships, such burdens, such self-abuse knows only pain and self-harm. When one looks at life, one sees a realm of many different perceptions. Some know only the joys it has to offer. Some know only the hells it holds within its gutters. Some have a reprieve only to face their feelings head on once again. For life is a constant battle. Its demands and conditions are ever-changing, ever-increasing, and its inhabitants forever at war with themselves and others. There are days when we will rise, days when we will fall, days when we will stumble, and days when we will be uncertain. There will be times when we will be tested about what we thought was true. There will be times when we see what made sense in the past actually never made sense. There will be times when we discover that what we thought we held dear was only an illusion. There will come a time when we will not know who to turn to, what to do, what to think, and how to feel. In those moments, we turn to those we deem worthy of our trust. In our times of need, we look inward as we feel threatened by the presence of the outside world. While trying to make sense of our conflicts, we create our own horrors and worst enemies. In such a time, the mind truly becomes our own prison. The fault that we come to realize is that we are weak, vulnerable, permeable. We are not as firm about the stance we originally took. We are not as sure of ourselves as we were when we first began our quest.

With time, we realize that we do not have what it takes to go at it alone. It is the illusion of self-reliance and independence that defeats us. Every individual believes that becoming their own person will be the panacea to all their problems. It is in navigating through our own problems and accomplishing our goals that we feel invincible. It is by being our own person that we feel that we can achieve any endeavor, no matter how difficult it may seem. We find comfort in only what we can do. Yet all we hear is what the masses project. All we hear are the opinions of those who know only what they want to hear. In return, we feel isolated, unsure of ourselves, convinced that we will have to be our own strong tower. Yet every soul must rest. Every warrior must find peace. But everyone must find comfort in others who understand. We all must find our group, those who can identify with us, relate to us. In that, we find solace. In that, we find comfort. And in that, we find what they call encouragement.

Encouragement. So many forget that we all make mistakes. So many forget that we are all but human. We all fall short of the understanding we seek. We all fall short of the one thing we need that will make us the best. And when we fall, we fall so hard that we become immobilized. It is as though we were almost destined to wind up in our predicament, and feel more naturally prone to failing than overcoming our afflictions. It is this innate sense of failure that makes rising above it seem almost impossible. And then, in overcompensating, we become nothing more than a dumb brute, charging head on at anything and everything we do. It is as if we have all this potential, yet are hindered by our natural affinity for a primitive nature. We float around and around trying to see where we should be in a world rampant with the boundless perspectives of others, with their own codes and creeds. For this world is too big for us to navigate, and its inhabitants too complex to understand. Yet we seek encouragement because all that we do, we cannot do alone. If we could, we would lead ourselves to our own destruction. If we could, we would fall prey to our own perspective, our own short-sightedness.

But what is encouragement? Is it but a word, or is it something more? Is it a concept that describes what people need to be strong? Does it describe a state that people go through to achieve their goals? Does it speak to the weak? The strong? The faint of heart? The willing? The able? The desperate? Is encouragement only for those who know pain, strife, defeat, loneliness? Is encouragement something we seek when we are in such a weakened state that we cannot propel ourselves forward? Is encouragement something that all people need? Is it something that we deny ourselves because we would view ourselves as weak? Is it the help we need, from others? Does encouragement let us know that we are not alone? That no matter the endeavor, the dream, the vision, that we are not alone? That there are others who feel how we feel, share what we share? Do we draw strength from it? Is that what encouragement is? Is it the affirmation of our beliefs from others? And from that affirmation, we find confidence to continue down the path we believe to be right?

There is so much pain in this world. There is so much misery that we all carry within us. There is so much hatred that lies within our hearts. People have so much ill will, so much malice, toward each other. It makes life unbearable. It makes hope a false reality, and makes living in this world harder. It makes fighting for something that is greater than us, better for us, that much harder. When you look at people, it seems that none care. You see such apathetic minds consumed by what they have chosen to accept rather than what they believe is worth fighting for. You see those who cannot sympathize with others since they have hardened their hearts to their emotions. You see none who can see what is wrong with the world, the times they live in, or themselves.

Living in such a time, is encouragement truly a thing of the past? Is the ability to sympathize/empathize with another in their current predicament and help them reach what they thought was not possible, is it gone? Can people no longer find aid in our human capacity for a warm embrace? There is no culture more diffused than ours, representing such a diversity of races, religions, skin colors, and, ethnicities, yet we cannot seem to find common ground? Are we so sophisticated, so refined, so bolstered by our modern-day advancements and achievements that we cannot offer aid, support, comfort, and encouragement to one another in our time of need? Was there not a society in which enemies showed respect to one another in their times of mourning? Was there not a time where rivals offered words of comfort to each other in their darkest hour? Was there not a time when people put aside their bitterness toward one another? When they understood how it could lead to the others demise, and, in the end, sought to build a bridge where others thought such a gap could never be filled? Have our emotions as people become so foreign to us that we do not know how to deal with them? Have we become so desensitized to the plight of others in the endeavor to find our own sense of individuality that we cannot stop to aid others? Have we become so lost in our quest for independence that we have hardened our hearts to the burdens of others? Have we forgotten that what we do affects others? Have we forgotten this thing called goodness? Have we forgotten this thing called benevolence? Have we forgotten that no matter how much we rise, we will fall? Have we forgotten that no matter how much we have overcome, we will always stumble? And have we forgotten that no matter how far we venture, how much we achieve, that no man, women, or child can ever make it on their own without the encouraging words of others?

Have we forgotten this thing called encouragement?

If one seeks encouragement, are they weak? If one seeks encouragement, are they strong? The weak hold encouragement in the highest esteem, since they cannot muster up enough strength to free themselves from the unconscious bonds, that weigh heavy on them. Some who are strong see encouragement as something they have no need for. Yet, others see it as the path to strength. For some come to understand that no one truly is invincible and that everyone needs help to achieve their goals by their own merit. Yet like all things, encouragement is something not understood by the masses. For every group is different, and every norm is not treated the same. Can any individual become all that they seek to be without hearing words of encouragement or feel the warmth and comfort it provides? Do even those considered to be the strongest possess so much fortitude that they can survive the harshness of the world and all the negativity found within the human heart by themselves? Or are they so broken, and bruised that they do not know how to accept nor interpret the kind words brought about by the embrace of encouragement? How does one reach such a broken soul? How does one penetrate such a broken heart? Are we as people contradictory in nature, so assured individually and collectively that we do not understand encouragement? Can we from a societal standpoint not accept the labels and norms brought about by bearing the stigma of needing encouragement? Have we come to shun such a fragile human condition that we do not understand what we sacrifice when we give up the ability to offer encouragement? Do we regard encouragement as something for the weak yet fail to realize that we are always in such a weakened state?

Thus, who is weak and who is strong: The one who seeks encouragement, or the one who is stronger because of it?

What is the downfall of encouragement? What is the downfall of seeking and embracing the warmth of those who feel as we feel? Just because you share with others the same beliefs, does not mean that what you believe in is true. Just because you find a group to call your own does not mean that all you believe in is true. It is the single-minded perspective of the group that often hinders an individual from broadening their point of view. It is the embrace by one group of a belief that hinders it from seeing the error of its ways. If encouragement is something all people seek, at what point does it become a hinderance? At what point does encouraging an individual hurt than rather than help them? At what point is encouragement too much? What then, is the downfall of encouragement? Is it the group-think? Is it the words of affirmation that pamper, tone down, the severity of the situation that the individual must face at some point? Does it trap a person in its warm comforts and blind them to the harsh reality that they must face at some point? Does it hinder them by making them forget why it is they sought encouragement… to eventually find their own strength? Are there then some things a person must face for themselves, without the words of encouragement? But how is that to be determined? At what point do we accept encouragement and at what point do we learn to move on without it while bearing its fruits?

Is encouragement a good thing? What if someone were encouraged to do something that was bad, went against the law, or would lead to their demise? Every group does not have the same goals or beliefs. Every group does not advocate for the same thing. Every group believes itself to be right and other groups wrong. Every group wishes their way of life and their beliefs to be adopted by all. Yet each group encourages something different. How does each group member determine if what they choose to believe in and accept according to the will of the group is a good thing? How does one know which behaviors and beliefs are worth encouraging and which should be dismissed? And how will we ever know what will come of it as time goes on?

Therefore, Is Encouragement a good thing?

If those who come after us are to be better than we are, they will need to be encouraged to see life and the ways of humanity in a way that we could not, and work toward what we never could … a better future. They will need to be encouraged as the path they take is full of risk, and an unknown risk is never understood until it exacts its price on those who dare to take it. If those who are to be better than us and to prosper, let alone have the strength to pick up where we left off, they must be encouraged. It is never easy to do better for those who have never known better. But we all need encouragement for we all struggle. While our struggles are different, we can come together in our vulnerable state. It is in this vulnerability that we can see in its purest form that which separates us from the person beside us. From there, we can understand just how weak we are, despite the cloak of strength we project in our daily lives. In that moment, we can see what it means to be human, what it means to fall, what it means to stumble. Yet in that, we can learn what it means to build, but build together. In that, we can be a comfort to others. In that we can find strength in others. In that, we learn that we are not alone in our struggles. In that, we learn that our battles are not just ours. In that, we find unity. And in that unity, we find strength. We find strength amongst others who share our beliefs in a world dominated by multiple perspectives. In finding our own strength, we find the will, the courage, the faith to continue to seek that which we hold true to our hearts. In that, we seek to become better for what we believe in. And in doing so, we become the change we wish to see in this world. In that, we find hope. Hope to make this world better for those who walk among us, and for those who will one day walk after us. In doing so, we become an example to those who will one day seek their path and what it means to them. And when they look to the past to see how those before them could ever venture into what others thought was impossible, they will find the encouragement necessary to continue on their journey to become their own individual, and be better because of it.

That is why encouragement is important. Not just for us, but for those who will come after us.

CHAPTER 20

APPRECIATION

f I could, I would go back in time. I wish I would not have taken for granted what my feeble little mind thought was a regular occurrence, but a privilege. If I could go back, knowing what I know now, I would do it all over again, but differently. How different would I be if I knew the circumstances of the situation back then? How much more grateful would I have been had I known what was really going on? Yet the past is something that can never be changed. All I can do is live in the present and hope and work towards a better future. As I live and breathe, as I walk this earth, as I begin to understand the world I live in and what governs it and what makes it go round and round, I'm beginning to understand how much I have to be grateful for. The living conditions of the human population are dire. To just meet the basic needs can be a struggle, can cost everything a person has at their disposal. Yet, we all want more. We want more of what we already have so that we do not have to fight for it every single day. And we long for what we want so that we can enjoy ourselves as we celebrate not having to constantly struggle financially.

Yet in all this struggle, in all this conflict, in all this chaos, we forget the little things. We forget the things we need the most. We forget the things we need to live. We forget the things that make us whole. We forget where we came from. We forget our friends and family. We forget the people who raised us, who took care of us. We forget the simple deeds done for us out of the love and kindness of others when we had nothing to offer. We forget the people who make life bearable, worth living when our current predicament reminds us of the living hell that we constantly face. We forget the little people. We forget the people we thought never mattered but do. We forget the smiles on their faces, the spots we used to hang out at, the oaths sworn to each other out of loyalty that bonded us back when we were idealistic kids with no clue about the harsh ways of the world. We forget the times spent together, the memories forged without us even knowing. Yet so many forget these things. So many forget these things because when they grew up, they lost their childish nature with its innocence and tender ideals as they accepted the world for what it is. Can you blame them? Can you blame each person for making this mistake since we are all guilty of it? Is it wrong if it is practical? To walk through life living this way, always forsaking that which matters most, is not a life worth living. To walk through life forgetting what made it worth living for each day is not life, but an unknown death not privy to us. Yet everyone has different beliefs about what is worth living. For each soul must search its own heart to understand what is worth appreciating. But what I speak of in terms of appreciation is what many have forsaken. What I speak of is of a spiritual and personal nature. What I speak of is a longing of the heart.

At first you do not see reflections of appreciation. All you see is mongrel on mongrel, mano on mano. All you see is a dog-eat-dog world. That is probably why so many do not know what appreciation is. When you step into the outside world, you see the survival of the fittest. You see one man topple over the other for table scraps. You see people being what they are, ruthless. There is so much to not only live for but be thankful for. The clothes on our back, the shoes on our feet, a roof over our heads, food on our table, the people in our lives, the people who really care for us. How about the air we breathe? The access to an abundance of goods and resources that we do not have to work for, but that is provided to us. The ability to choose our own fates. The ability to have access to a wealth of knowledge. The ability to choose for ourselves what we get to do with our lives. The ability to wake up every morning without the overarching fear of death. The luxury of a society better than the ones of old. The ability to use our body functionally.

There is so much that we take for granted that we do not stop to appreciate. We get so caught up in the pursuit of our own desires, that we never take the time to think to ourselves what is it that we should be grateful for. We are so focused on ourselves that we never take the time to understand the plight of others. We never take the time to be thankful in our hearts for what we have. But what I speak of is not just material possessions but things of a mental and spiritual nature. We never take the time to truly appreciate the things that will one day fade away. We never take the time to give back to those who have given to us. We never take the time to be grateful that we made it to see another day. We never take the time to appreciate the person who is always next to us, beside us in our darkest hour. We never take the time to be grateful for the opportunity to be the change we seek to be. We never understand, in the moment, that we have a chance to be the change we always longed for, but never imagined growing up.

What a blessing it would be to be more than what we thought we were capable of. Yet so many fail to consider their potential and act on it. We forsake it for capitalistic, economic, social, even political pursuits. But which matters more? With every day that passes, we never realized how much we have survived. With each day that passes, a life ends. Each day that passes is someone's last. With each day, a soul is laid to rest, never to walk the mortal plane again. Yet with each day, a life is born. It knows not why it is here, but it is. With each day, a life is ushered into this world. And with each day, there is a spark of hope. With each life that begins a-new, a new age is ushered in that can be better than the one before it. Within that new life beats a heart. Within that heart lies a soul. Within that soul is a spark for decency, a spark to someday be the one to change the natural order of things for a better world, a world that those before never knew could exist. When we are in the thick of things, we think there is not much to be thankful for, to give praise to the almighty for. Yet there is more to appreciate than what we believe. There is more to celebrate than we believe. There is more to give thanks to the highest power than we believe. Despite our living conditions on this earth, there is much to appreciate. It starts with everyone honestly caring, and working every day to become the person they fantasized about when growing up, could become that person. It is never too late.

Yet, what is appreciation? Why should one appreciate something or have appreciation for others? Does it make them a good person? Does it make them righteous? Does it make them somewhat decent? How does one show their appreciation for someone or something? What classifies as an act of appreciation? Is it appreciative if it comes from the heart? But what if someone's heart is full of hate? What if someone's hearts is full of malice? What if someone believes in is the destruction of all things? If the goal is a malevolent one, how can they appreciate something of that nature? Is that all that they are, the actions they envision or commit to achieve that goal? Is appreciation the same for everyone? Is a part of basic common ground that all people agree when it comes to showing appreciation for someone or something? Can appreciation as a concept be understood by all people? It speaks to people of all creeds, colors, religions, beliefs. Can it be a unifying factor that can bring people together? Can it be something that allows people to treat each other as equals? Is that hard? Is that possible? Or is that impossible?

How different would life be, would people be if we appreciated each other? Despite our nature to always be at odds with the person who is different from us, can we accept, and appreciate them for what they can offer? Is it possible to appreciate people for who they are rather than what their worth to society is? Is it possible for men and women to appreciate and accept each other? Is it possible for men and women to have their differences but come together and love each other in spite of these differences? Is it possible for each of us to accept ourselves? Why is it that we as people, can never appreciate the other? We like to believe that we are of a benevolent nature, yet we are always at odds with the people we deem odd. How can that be?

What will it take for each person to appreciate the other? It is impossible for every person to hold the same amount of respect for the other if they do not know them, so what is the next best alternative? How can people come to appreciate each other for who they are rather than what they may have that is of economic or capitalistic value?

Can we achieve it for ourselves rather than as a society? Can we each find what we appreciate the most and live our life better because of it? Can we become more grateful, more thankful, humbler even when we understand how much we must be appreciative for? Can we be better human beings than what we were yesterday? Can we be batter people than the ones who came before us? Can we be the agents of change, the change ourselves that we wish we had when we were young? Can we learn to appreciate the people in our lives, those we cherish, as well as those who we never thought about but who made a positive difference in our lives? When we come to appreciate what we have, can we learn to stop wasting our lives trying to be someone we are not, and instead become the epitome of our own individual?

Can we ever learn to truly be grateful, appreciative?

Will we ever learn to appreciate what we truly possess, whatever that is?

We all fall short of caring. We all fall short of understanding. We all fall short of being thankful, grateful for what we have. As each day passes, we forget what it is that allows us to do what we can do. As each day passes, we take for granted the goods and resources at our disposal provided to us by our own hands, community, and nation. With each day of luxury, we forget what life is like on a basic level. With each moment that we draw breath, we forget how different life would be without the ability to breathe. On some level, there is something that each person needs to be whole but takes for granted. For some, it is family. For others, it is friendship. For others, it is the ability to care for others. There are so many things that people as a whole take for granted. We take for granted the freedoms that we have. We take for granted our comfortable lifestyle. We take for granted the various choices we have that others make for us that are for our well-being. We take for granted the various outlets of human life that are at our disposal yet and are always available. We take for granted our loved ones, our friends, our families. We take for granted those we see on a regular basis.

Most importantly, we take for granted our own lives. We as human beings are such selfish creatures. It is all about us in the end and never about others. We each want the whole world in our hands, the attention of others at our very command, and we are foolish enough to think that if we possessed it, it would not corrupt us. For example, we ask for freedom. We ask, fight, and advocate for the ability to be our own individual and have our own form of self-expression. Yet what happens when we do? What happens when we have all that we have fought so hard to achieve? Many, if not all, of us misuse that freedom and very few become better for the journey they embark on with the freedom they possess. Many fall to the corruption brought about by temptations and the illusion that their freedom of self-expression grants them as a human being. In our moments of victory, we forget what we lost, what we sacrificed to get to where we thought was impossible. In our daily walk on the path we deem true to our own perspective, we forget what life was like without it. With complacency, we forget what it meant to struggle. With all that we possess, with all that we fight for, with all that was given to us without us ever having to work for it, so many never come to understand just how fortunate they are to have what they have and be able to choose from the very things they can choose from. And it is a shame that people, no matter how smart and wise, may never understand what they truly possess.

In generations past, with struggle came hardship. And with hardship, came a sense of appreciation for what we had rather than what we could achieve.

CHAPTER 21

PERSEVERANCE

There is something mysterious, yet powerful about the nature of humanity. It started out as a primitive species with little to no cognitive reasoning or comprehension. Yet it somehow managed to build empires, forge nations, win wars, utilize its natural surroundings to the highest degree. It created fields of study dedicated to the understanding of the world and its higher order. With each generation came an innovation, an invention greater than the one before it. With each era, came a different perspective, a new insight into the inner world of the human being that shaped the world around it. With time, theories became reality, equations became blueprints from the human mind that would shape society for ages to come. Yet, all of that came from cave dwellers and hunter-gatherers.

Within each human being lies something dormant. Within each person is an ability that is unknown to them. It could not be put into words even if they were aware of it because it, cannot be describe. Yet they know how they feel when they experience it. It is an ability that comes to us in our time of need, almost as if it were put in place for that specific instant in a time of crisis. It is an ability, a form of expression, whose core is hard to evaluate. It goes deeper than empirical evidence; it is something that can be explained by neither quantitative nor qualitative data. It is something that can only be felt more than it can be defined. Even if it could easily be put into words, its true meaning is understood only when a person experiences it for themselves. What is weird about the ability is that it has always been there.

At every major point in human history, observed and unobserved, it has been there. Without it, humanity would not be where it is today. In every social movement that changed human thought, it was there. At the discovery of every endeavor that broke boundaries people thought were impossible, it was there. From the cave dweller to the ancient sages, and from the ancient sages to modern man, it was there. From all the hell that was wrought from war, slavery, and all that was evil in people, humanity always survived because of it and became better because of it. Every person has the ability but does not understand it to the same degree. It can make a person, forge them into something greater with time and patience. A person can become better because of it, or crack, wither, and fade if they are not willing to bear the burdens it requires. It is the one key difference that separates one person from the next. It is something that must be experienced by each person on their own if they are to possess it for themselves. Many will claim they have it, but who they are and what they have been through will be the judge of whether the claim is true. With time, a person who possesses this ability can be something more than they thought was possible. But if they are ever willing to become something more, something greater, something better than what they once were, they must first endure, struggle, and be tested. What is it that I speak of?

What I speak of is perseverance.

To persevere is no mean feat. To persevere is no simple thing. The difficulties each person will face in life blocks them, hinders them from becoming their own individual. Therefore, each person's journey to become who they believe they are destined to be will unfold differently. The path they will take is one filled with challenges and obstacles. What they will face will test them beyond what they know. For some, it is a test of endurance, how much they are willing to take to achieve what they believe to be true and worth living for. For some, it will be a test of character. For some, a test of faith. For some, a test of skill. For others, a test of intelligence. Yet at some point along each person's journey, all that they know will fail them. At some point, what they thought they knew to be true will be the very source of their confusion and frustration. When all we know fails us, we collapse. We try to make sense of the situation, but we cannot because the validity of what we thought was true is questionable. For there will come a time when we will not know what to do. Perseverance will lead us to anger, confusion, doubt, fear, and other negative emotions. And, spiritually, it will break us. It will crack us open and reveal to us what little significance we have. It will prove to us how small we are, how futile our actions were, how meaningless our beliefs are. At such a time, our mind becomes our greatest prison. At that moment, the definition of depression cannot begin to describe what it is we feel. We feel low, but we cannot explain it. We feel so low that we feel we can never get back up. We feel so low that we believe we will never find something in this world that makes sense, something to live for. We feel so low that we just accept our fate. In that moment, we feel that no one can ever understand our plight. We become so deeply engrained in that deep fallen state that we feel we can never rise above it. There are so many things in life that we as people can explain, but we do not know the weight of our words because we have never for ourselves experienced what it means.

Many tell us to hold their heads up in times of need, but how many have endured a true burden? How many have been to the depths of their core, to the very essence of their soul and seen themselves in their true form? How many have been questioned, challenged to their core as to what they believed was true? How many have tried to live their life by challenging their beliefs and seeing the folly of them? How many can describe to themselves how they felt when their reason for living was questioned to the point where they did not know what to believe in anymore? It is much harder than you think to endure. So many make light of a heavy situation. So many dismiss as unimportant something that holds so much meaning. At some point in our lives, all that we know will fail us. For those who rely on their skill and physical prowess to guide them through a situation, it will fail them. For those who rely on their intellect, intelligence will at some point fail them. For those who walk with a higher power, their faith will be called into questioned at some point and, will one day fail them. Many will run, some will cower, some will fight but to no avail. So, what do you do in such times of crisis? Do you endure? Do you persevere?

But what does it mean to persevere?

What does it mean to persevere? Does it mean to simply stand by as the struggles of life weigh down upon you? Does it mean to just stand idle and do nothing with the hope that what ails you will someday pass? What does it mean to persevere? How does one seek perseverance? Is it by the trials of life that we learn what it means? Is it by the experiences that we go through that we develop a sense of what it means to persevere? Each person will go through their own struggles. Each person will have to go through something specific to them if they are to achieve their goal. Therefore, will every person come to have the same level of understanding of what it means to have perseverance? And even if every person will someday achieve their goals, will they ever have the same level of understanding of what it means to persevere?

So, is perseverance a universal act? Is it the same for all people? Or is that challenge, learning how to persevere, individually? Does it look the same on the outside? Does the true fight to persevere occur in the human realm, the outer world? Or does it happen in the inner world of people? Is one more stressful than the other? Is one harder to achieve than the other? On the outside is it so simple to persevere? On the inside, in our minds and our hearts, is it so simple to just persevere? For perseverance is something we experience when we are at our wits end, when all that we do fails us, when all that we know fails us. Will every person go through their own trials? Will some have a better understanding than others? Will some try to cheat the journey? Will some tap in and tap out of the journey? Will some be truthful to themselves, experience the journey for what it is and seek to be genuinely better because of it? But what will it produce? What are the fruits of perseverance? Will a person come to have a better understanding as they persevere beyond what they know or what they thought was true? Will a person become worse if they do not persevere on their own to become their own individual? What makes perseverance good and what makes it bad? At what point does perseverance become good or bad? Will every person who experiences hardship, who comes to endure on their own, struggle to become better? Will they become stronger in what they believe in? Will they become weaker in what they believe in? Will they understand that which they seek?

But how long is such a journey? How long must one suffer, fight, endure, persevere if they are to find what they are looking for or understand what they seek? A day? A week? A month? A year? A decade? Half a century? A lifetime? Can people wait that long? Is such a journey worth taking at that point? Is such a pursuit worth waiting that long for the answer that may never be true? Will some find what they are looking for more than others? Will others have to wait longer? Will some know what they were looking for on their death bed? Will some realize it before it is too late? Or will they ever realize it at all?

What is perseverance?

What does it mean to persevere?

Why should one persevere?

There will come a time in every person's life where they will question for themselves what it means to live, what it means to be their own being, what in life is worth living for, and whether their beliefs are true. There are no definitive answers to such pursuits, nor is there an answer that will satisfy every soul. For what a person truly seeks is within themselves, and it is up to them to find it. But if they ever decide to take such a journey and do so honestly, they will have to endure. They may never be satisfied with the answer they get, but must learn to accept what they come to find at that point in time. As they embark on this journey, they will be tested. Tested in ways they never knew they could be tested in. They will be tested in what they believe in, what they thought they believed, and what they seek to believe.

Eventually, they will come to a point in their journey where they can no longer rely on their intellect. They will come to a point where they can no longer rely on their rational side, their ability to use reason. They cannot rely on what they once thought was true as such a thing comes into question. At some point, they will question if what they do has meaning. All that they try to justify, they no longer can as their usual explanations are now the source of their confusion. In that moment of confusion, it is human nature to find comfort in whatever will alleviate them of their pain. But to do so before the journey of finding oneself is complete would do more harm than good. So, what do they do? Question the who, what, where, when, how, and why of their beliefs. Question it to better understand it. But they must persevere to find the answer, for it reveals itself only with time and patience. It may take days, weeks, months, years, decades, or even one's lifetime. But if they are willing to seek the truth, they will endure. For the key to unlocking life's mysteries comes to us when we are ready to receive it, not when we want it to. But we will never reach the end if we do not start. We will never be more than what we are now if we do not work toward it. We will never be the change we wish to be if we never make the effort within ourselves.

If we never have the perseverance to endure the hard times, we will never get to experience, enjoy, and understand the good times.

CHAPTER 22

SIMPLICITY

We live life driven by the illusion of extravagance. It has always been the desire of every soul to have more, to be more, to want more. We all want luxury, desire luxury, for what we think it will bring us. We think of the lavish lifestyle that makes people feel like kings and queens. Those who live this lifestyle can partake in their desired activities because of the goods, resources, and time available to them. In this way, they are distinct from others who must work all day. While others suffer, they thrive. While others collapse just trying to gather table scraps, they live a rich and spoiled.

In the back of our minds, the fantasies we create to cope with the harsh truth of our current predicament are all we have. For we each long to have what few will ever possess in their lifetime. We dream about others beneath our feet, at our command, at our servitude. We each think of how joyful we would be if we were the center of attention, the one everyone else feeds into. We each think to ourselves and how different we would be if we had power, control, and dominance over others. The idea of being able to impose our will over others brings us nothing but bliss. The very thought of being part of a social group that can regularly engage in activities only granted to a certain few, to those of distinct privilege, is every heart's true aspiration. But that is what we most desire, distinction. The ability at any moment to remind others that we stand higher than them. The constant reminder that we are special, and others are not. It is that distinction that grants us separation from others. It is that separation that grants us a sense of privilege. And it is that privilege that gives us a sense of power. No matter where we are on the social ladder, we all desire fame, glory, prestige, and luxury. The knowledge that not only will our basic needs always be provided for, but that we can express and embrace our heart's deepest desires is one of the greatest temptations and illusions of all time.

The feeling of living life in a way that we may never experience again is nothing but tempting. It may be vexing and, intoxicating in the long run, but in our hearts it is forever addicting. It is a drug more powerful than any physical substance, for it reaches the heart, not the body. It stimulates the mind, reinforces that fantasy we have always had but told ourselves was a fairy tale. Yet that illusion, the idea that such a thing is possible and may be within our grasp, is enough to give even the dead life. But then what? What comes after? Can we sustain such a desire before it kills us? Can we sustain something we know is intoxicating yet addicting? Can we sustain it, even if it is only good for the short term? But who can resist such temptation? Who can resist the chance to live life to the fullest and have whatever soul has always wanted? Who is of such character to say no and live life in their current condition? For what then is the pro that comes with the con? What is the counter acting agent that can balance such a fantasy, if such a thing exists? How then does one live like a king or queen while seeing life through the eyes of a servant?

———

I find it to be simplicity.

———

The simple. Many regard simplicity as something not worth having until they are old and have nothing to live for. Many see simplicity as the enemy of progress and change. Many think that nothing good can ever come about by being simplistic in nature. It is a dichotomy when you look at it. Those who are simplistic in nature have something more than what most people can understand. They are often envied because they are satisfied to their heart's desire in ways that most of us can't comprehend. We respect them because they never frown about their situation, yet we think to ourselves that they can have so much more. We put ourselves in their shoes to see what drives them, and we eventually become perplexed. We ask ourselves how such a person can exist. How can they live with their actions not guided by ambition, drive, passion, vigor, energy? How can they have a fulfilled existence without, seeking something that is tangible in nature? What do they possess that is intangible yet gives them fulfillment, unlike others who suffer for not having enough physical possessions? Is it a sense of pride? A sense of accomplishment that others on the outside do not see? Simplicity as a concept eludes many of us because we do not understand how not wanting to achieve something that is held in high regard can satisfy a person.

It is often the young who fail to understand simplicity because of their hunger for new experiences. Youth brings forth growth, and that growth spurs the desire to become self-reliant and independent. For the young know nothing but their own ambitions, their own desires, their own fantasies. That is why when they look at the old, there is disdain in their eyes and a sense of disappointment in their hearts. Because the young do not understand what it means to be old, set in your ways, and complacent with where you are in life. That is why those who are simplistic in nature are often seen as ignorant. And when the old look at the young, they feel a sense of shame, regret even. Shame and regret in the sense that they wish they were once again filled with passion, energy, vigor, and desire. Yet older people also wish that the young were not so bold, headstrong, ferocious, and impulsive. But when we are young, we dream big. We dream so big that we forget that which is small. And when we forget that which is small, we forget what made life what it once was. Youth allows us to go places that only our minds and hearts can take us; their desires make the simplicity of life seem futile. Yet when we forget simplicity, we make mistakes brought about by our own selfishness and greed. When we think we are better than what we once knew, where we once lived, we think we are destined for great things. So we venture into the unknown to seek something and the possibilities of what can be. In doing so, we try to make our fantasies a reality. We try to live life to such an extent that we can become more than what we were, even blossom into the person we were meant to become.

What is simplicity? Those who work every day for less than they should know it better than the people who feast like kings. Those who have always been taken care for, who have never wanted for anything, see simplicity as a foreign concept. It is a commodity you cannot buy because it is not for sale.

Yet what is simplicity in a general sense? Is it a way of life? Is it something you can easily obtain based on the way you live or how you were raised? Is it something that one group of people possess more than another? Is it a human quality that speaks to one's character? Is it something that only the elderly possesses as they look back on their life? Is it something they come to understand with time? Do they see all that they have obtained, accomplished, and fought for, and begin to understand that some of the things they sought to possess, they never needed? With that understanding, do the elderly become grateful for what they have? And do they then accept themselves for who they are and how they live? Or do they then have contempt for what they have, when it is so little compared to what others possess? Do they ever come to an understanding that what they possess is far greater than material possessions?

Is simplicity something that the young can possess? They are driven by ambition, desire, a hunger to leave their mark on this world, a capability and willingness to shape the future so that when they die, others will remember them for how they lived. Will the youth of tomorrow understand what it means to be simple in nature? Will they know what that means? Is simplicity something they will grow capable of desiring with age? Can they quench that desire to want it all, to be all they can, to have all they ever wanted? Can they satisfy their thirst for what the old can no longer maintain? Do the aspirations pf youth make them stupid? Does that make them dangerous? Does that make them prey on others? Does that blind them to the truth of reality? Does that in fact make them more susceptible to the trappings of the world? Do they then become victims of their own ambitions, trapped by the temptations of their own illusions?

So, what then is simplicity? Is it a difference in perspective? Is it a state of mind? Is it an understanding of the soul? Is it something that each person will one day come to understand for themselves? Is it something that each person will need in their life as they get older? Is it relevant to how we live life? Is it necessary? Is it the one thing that will stop us from going too far in our pursuits? Can it save us from going past the point of no return? Can it help us, redeem us? Can it be a blessing to us even if we do not know it at the time? Or can simplicity be a curse that hinders us from becoming all we can when we are fueled by ambition, determination, and drive?

Is simplicity a good thing or a bad thing?

Where is simplicity found? Is it found amongst the commoner? Is it found in the ruler of nations? Can those with power to create and enact change and the ability to destroy, know what simplicity is? Is the peasant simplistic? Is the servant simplistic? Is the gambler simplistic? Is the revolutionary simplistic? Is the farmer simplistic? Is the business mogul simplistic? Is the governor simplistic? Is the envoy simplistic? Is the teacher simplistic? Is the sage simplistic? Can simplicity be found amongst only the old? Can the spoiled brat learn simplicity? Is simplicity an easily understood concept? How is it learned? Is it leaned through struggle? Can it be taught through academics? Can it be understood by one's upbringing? What does it take for a person to understand what it means to be simple in nature?

Yet, for all the intangible rewards it can bring, why should one be simple? No great change ever came about by being simple. No one ever became famous by being simple. No person ever left their mark on the world by being simple. No deed that went on to change the world and how people live in it was ever simple. If people respond more to the unorthodox than they do to the conventional, what good thing ever comes about by being simple? Who recognizes the simple? If no great change comes about by being simplistic, why should we be so? If being simple means no longer setting one's sights on the future, being closer to the end of life than the beginning, is it really a positive thing?

It is amazing how the young neglect simplicity for lavishness and extravagance, yet as they get older they wish they had known what it was. Why then is it that simplicity is something not desired by most when it is in fact something worth having? Why do people neglect simplicity when they need it, yet desire it when it is too late? Does simplicity yield fruit, is it ultimately worthwhile? Is there anything worth more than money, power, fame, riches, splendor, glory, prestige, and praise a person when one can possess simplicity at heart? Is simplicity really what many people think it is, this inability to be fueled by passion, vigor, and a sense of purpose in life? Is it something more than what the consensus is? Is that understanding something that can be universal to all people if they apply themselves to its teachings?

For how different life would be if people were more simplistic in nature rather than chasing extravagance and lavishness.

Why should one be simplistic in nature?

There is no right answer to such a question. For in each heart, in each mind, and within each soul is the desire to venture into the unknown and become the epitome of who they can be. It is in adventure, thrill, the trenches even that we find ourselves. It is the constant pressure brought about by our experiences that sharpens us and hardens us to be able to bear more than what we once could. Doing so allows us to gain more insight into ourselves, to see if we have what it takes to reach our mark. There is no way to tell the generations of tomorrow not to dream big and be all they can be. There is no way to tell a person so filled with hunger, passion, desire, along with the determination and will to make such a dream come true, to be simple. There is no way to tell a soul so beat down, and let down not to dream big. Humanity never benefitted by being simplistic. It was unconventional warfare that won the battle and, ultimately, the war. It was innovation brought about by creativity and genius that advanced human-ity out of the Stone Age. It was thinking outside the box that allowed the once known cave-dwellers and hunter-gatherers to become the kings, queens, pharaohs, and Caesars that came to rule the world.

Human beings are more sophisticated in their nature than their ances-tors were. We may have advanced in a short amount of time compared to those who came before us. But no matter how many times we plan, we always manage to make the same mistakes they did, just in a different way. While we are capable of advanced thought, and greater refinement than we once were, at the end of the day our needs are still simple: sex, hun-ger, warmth, shelter, attention, affection, and understanding. All of which describes humanity in its entirety. While we may be more than we once were, at any moment we can slip right back to who we used to be. While we can have all the material possessions in the world, what we truly seek, money can never buy. Money can buy you a house, but it can't give you a home. Money can buy you sex, but it can't give you love. Money can buy you friends, but it can't give you a family.

While there is nothing wrong with aiming for the stars, we must be reminded that we can only live on the planet called earth.

CHAPTER 23

STRENGTH

What is it that drives us? When we face an existential crisis, what gives us a reason to live? What is it that an individual will give their life to find a reason to live for and a purpose for their actions? What is worth living for on earth before we forever fade into the unknown? What can be so worthy of our time, our energy, worth more than all the resources in the world that we would sacrifice all material possessions just to achieve it? What is worth more than what all men deem desirable by their own standards? What is worth more than money, power, fame, riches, glory, splendor, adventure, influence, admiration from others? What could be more worthy in our eyes than the attainment of diamonds, emeralds, rubies, sapphires, gold, silver, or any precious element that others would kill just to have? What could satisfy our fleeting existence with the mere amount of breath we have on this earth? What do people really want out of life? What is it that every heart, mind, and soul desires while they live in the realm of recorded history? What can bring everyone that has drawn breath, that currently draws breath, and will one day draw breath more pleasure than anything else? With all the time we have on this earth before we die, what can we commit ourselves to that which we deem an honorable cause? What can we obtain for ourselves that we can be proud of as we contemplate the meaningfulness of our existence on our death-bed? When we are young, what is worth having?

When we are young, we look to commit ourselves to anything that we can identify with, anything that we deem worthwhile and that will give us a sense of adventure. We look to involve ourselves in something enriching that, we can reflect upon as we age. Its in those moments where we can say that life was worth living. It is in those moments that we wanted to find not only adventure, but ourselves. When we are young, we committed ourselves to anything that gave us a thrill, but was that good for us? Was that something we can honestly say was productive for us? Did it further advance us down the path we were meant to go on? Did it propel us to become the person we were meant to become? As we age, we reflect on the things we did in our youth. We think about how stupid we were to consider doing such things we now find grotesque. We reflect on how impulsive we were, riding life like a roller coaster and moving with every twist and turn at full throttle. Yet we always ask ourselves, was it worth it? Did we ever find the sense of meaning we were looking for? Did we find our calling?

For what is the meaning of life as we draw closer to death? What is the purpose of existence if we will know the abyss longer than we will know life itself? Why live, seek mundane pursuits if we will never exist long enough to see the fruits of our labor? What is the purpose of life if we will not remember in totality the sum of our actions? Why live if we will die? Why move about if we will forever lie still? For what endeavor could possibly be worth living if we cannot do it forever? What goal, what vision, what dream, what fantasy could be worth living for or acting out if it may never come to pass? Why live if we cannot give our existence meaning? Why live for momentary things if they hold no value in the end? Why gather and collect worldly goods if we cannot take them with us to the place where we know not where, we go? For what in life is worth living for while we live? Is our pursuit, the journey we embark on for ourselves, a testament to what we believe is worth living for as we draw closer to our eternal death? And is it worth living for as we choose to pursue it? For what is worth living for as we live?

At the beginning of our lives, we must rely on others to take care of us as we cannot take care of ourselves. At such a point, we are physically, psychologically, and spiritually gullible, dependent. As we grow, we will believe everything and anything just to survive. We will do whatever it takes to belong to the social group. But why? Some say we know no better. Others say we explore different aspects of life to better understand the world around us. But I say that we are weak. We do anything and accept anything because we are weak. But the weakness stems from ignorance and arrogance. We are weak physically because we cannot defend ourselves against the advances from others to reject what they offer. We are weak mentally to resist the urge and temptations brought about by the allure of something we do not understand. And we are weak spiritually as we lack an understanding of what we see missing in ourselves that we believe we can find in others. At some point, every individual will come to face such a dilemma. They will face a dilemma of the soul (aka an existential crisis). At some point, every person will have to ask themselves with as much honesty as they can muster, what is worth living for.

Every heart, every soul yearns for something that will propel them to be more, have more, and obtain more than those around them. For some it is money, for others it is fame. For some, it is the roar of the crowd, praises from the masses. Yet on an individual level, we desire something we can gain only on our own that others will praise us for. We desire something to that will make us more than our physical form. With this, we find our own independence. With this, we find our calling. With this, we can lead our own lives and venture ahead in time to become all that we will one day be. The ironic thing about life is that we never know how to get there on our own, yet we all need to start the journey. But what is it that we seek while we live? What is it that is worth having that no material possession can give us? We all seek something, something that is universal to every social class. The rich seek it, the poor seek it, the working class seek it. Some deem it a gift. With this very gift, we can make all our dreams a reality. With this gift, we can build what others thought was impossible. With this gift, we can venture into what we think is the unknown and not be afraid of it. With this gift, life becomes easier to bear as we hit the bumps in the road that we cannot foresee. It makes living worthwhile. It makes all that we do easy as it allows us to see it done by our own hands, by way of our own merit.

As we get older, we hear it more and more from those we deem successful. We see it throughout history by those who are remembered for possessing it. We see it emanate from others as they command respect for it. We see it come from others as those around them are naturally attracted to them. Some are even worshipped for it, admired for it, extoled for it. People all over the world of all races, creeds, cultures, and ways of life understand what can come from it as they begin to learn what it means and what can happen once they do. As you get older, you see that it is a force of nature that all creatures live by. All can have it, few obtain it, and fewer still will become better for it as they walk in it. It dazzles us as we see what it can do for a person as they live and breathe. We see what a person can be because of it as they understand what it means and how it affects the world around them. As we get older and become wiser, we desire it as it shapes the world around us as if we have the power of God himself. We tell ourselves that if we possess it, we can become the very epicenter that all things revolve around. It is that one thing that all people desire and live for.

Not power, but strength

———————————

The ability to create, the ability to destroy, frightens us yet excites us. The capacity to be responsible for the decimation of the old or forsaken, yet the power to be responsible for the construction of the new and desirable, is something that tempts all people. The ability to create change, enact change with just one's words, is intoxicating, and alluring. The ability to not be bound by the norms, customs, societal institutions, and processes that govern most is a feeling that one can ascend to, to the very heights of the heavens. The ability to be boundless, formless, shapeless, misunderstood by so many, yet command all, is something that can make one feel as if they are God. To have control over life and death itself, the ability to deconstruct and reconstruct, the ability to take form yet be formless, is something that perplexes all yet is desired by all. The ability to have power, influence, control, and dominance over what others deem desirable is entrancing. It speaks to us at our very core. It speaks to the part of us that seeks to be strong. A part of all of us desires strength; it is natural to desire something that helps one to overcome their enemies as well as their afflictions.

And that is what the thought of strength does to a person. But strength also speaks to our weakness. It speaks to our state of helplessness. It speaks to how little, how insignificant, how irrelevant we are. It reminds us how weak we are in the reality of the passing moment yet reveals how much we yearn for a shred of power because we are weak. It reminds us that even with all we possess, all that we are, how distinguished we may be to others or in our own fields of expertise, we are fragile. The desire for strength reminds us of the constant struggles brought about by our fragile state. The very notion of having strength is a constant reminder of how close to absolute power over others each person could come to, yet be forever reminded that they are nothing, but mortals bound to an ever-fading plane of existence.

Yet the concepts of power, control, influence, and dominance are something we all desire to understand. In such things, we see how we can be the kings and queens we are in our psyches. In our minds, we see how having strength can propel us to be the Alpha. People desire to be the leader of the pack, the epicenter around which all things happen. It is such figures who command respect. It emanates from them as if they were born to lead. It is an unspoken language understood by all who follow them. From such figures, we are given the epitome of what strength looks like. From such individuals, we are given a description of what inner strength could forge a person into. It is that image, that mental description, that becomes engrained in our minds. It leads us to seek the strength we believe will allow us to one day rise beyond all others and take our place where we believe we should be… above them. It is that depiction and that illusion of strength that drives us, guides us, and gives us reason to live. It is enticing, it knows no boundaries as it speaks to all creatures from all walks of life. It is not communicated through the common tongue yet is understood by all. It is a universal constant that the weak die and the strong live. Yet like all things sought by humanity, our greatest ambition is the source of our demise. It is the things we long for the most that destroy us in the end. For it is the pursuit of strength that detaches one from what they once were. It is the possession of strength that makes one forget their natural state of being. It is the quest to obtain what one deems to be strength that makes one forsake all those who do not pursue such a goal. And it is the failure of the seeker to understand what strength is. Ultimately, they will be consumed by the very thing they wish to achieve in the end.

Of all the attributes, qualities, and virtues sought by man, none are misunderstood more than strength. What makes strength misunderstood is the use of it by the individual who claims to have it. The brute sees strength for how it can augment their physical form. The weak do not understand strength as it is something foreign to their nature. The warrior regards their level of strength based on their level of physical skill or martial prowess. The intellectual regards strength as a feat of the mind, defeating others before the battle is fought, outsmarting their opponent without their opponent even realizing it. Some see it as form of encouragement and replace it with empowerment. Many see strength as a source of power. Many who seek strength only seek the power to destroy. Many are so consumed by their own weakness and frailty that they exhaust the strength they possess but are unaware of. With strength comes power, with power comes the ability to create change around us and the change we seek to make a reality is a testament to what lies within our hearts.

The ultimate downfall of most people who seek strength is that they will never understand it, yet they claim to possess it. Everyone is trapped by their own bias; they are a slave to their own perspective. They are the greatest obstacle in their own path. The greatest lie everyone tells themselves is that they can reach the highest level of knowledge, wisdom, skill, intellect, and understanding, and they are the best. In our pursuit of strength, we fall prey to this illusion. The moment we gain a shred of power, a better understanding than the one we had before, reach a higher level than the one we thought at one point was the highest we could achieve, we are hit with an overwhelming feeling of superiority. We then think we know something or are capable of doing something that makes us better than those around us. In that moment of enlightenment, we fall as we rise higher, we lose just as we gain, we take two steps back as we take one step forward. The hardest thing about strength is that it is essential yet ambiguous to every human being. Some believe strength to be a feat of the body. Others believe strength to be a feat of the mind. And some believe strength to be housed within the human spirit. The difference in perspective reveals itself in the outward expression of what one deems strength. It is our understanding of the strength we claim to have that shows us and reveals to others how important it is to us. For such a misunderstood concept, there are many takes on how it should be comprehended or used. For some, strength is the ability to destroy. Some see strength in the ability to maintain, preserve. And some see strength in the ability to create, to establish, to build something new and leave something behind that is essential for humanity. But who is right and who is wrong on the interpretation of strength and the use of it? Who is right and who is wrong in how one should come to understand the source of strength? Who is right and who is wrong when they make the claim that what they possess is strength and not a fraction or an illusion of it? Who has the right to say that what they possess is strength? And how is one seen as possessing strength?

For what is this misunderstood concept, what is strength?

Where does strength come from? Is strength divine? Does it come from God, a heavenly entity/deity? Does strength come from the universe itself? Does one have to worship a being greater than themselves to receive the strength to do whatever they believe to be worth their time and effort? Does it come from the human body? Is it housed within the cells of the individual, their various muscle groups? Is strength a result of a sophisticated use of one's body to defend oneself, to protect oneself, overcome others by way of physical combat? Is strength the physical ability to impose one's will, dominance, control, and desires over others by way of physical feats alone? Is strength something found in the mind? Is it a result of intellectual prowess? Does strength come by way of the human spirit? And if so, how? Is it the ability to never give up? Is strength the ability to persevere, to endure hardship when one's skill, knowledge, wisdom, core beliefs, and intelligence fails them? Is strength of the spirit the ability of an individual to find their own voice, their own courage when they believed they never possessed any at all? Is strength of the spirit housed in the form of will and fear? Is it the ability to look death, tyranny, oppression in the eye, yet firmly hold one's ground? Is strength the ability to heal, to sympathize, to empathize? Is it the ability to go where others cannot, despite knowing that you will be an outcast, a foreigner to those you live among? Is strength the ability to see what others cannot, to have a perspective that challenges what they believe to be true? Is strength restraint? Is strength found in the form of character? Is morality a source of strength? Is being ethical, an individual of principles for the sake of being a better human being a sign of strength? Is being more than one's baser instincts a sign of strength? Or is it something one possesses within themselves, something that makes one who they are? How do people, past and, present, comprehend the misunderstood concept of strength? How do they interpret its meaning and proper use? If strength is not universal, is it the source of an individual's true capabilities, a form of self-expression?

What is strength?

What does it mean to be strong?

Why should one possess strength?

Within human beings is a contradictory nature, the ability to both create and destroy. Within them is the power to generate life and the ability to take it. They possess this because it is the very state of their being (first life, then death). Yet due to their lack of understanding of what strength is, how to use it, and what it means to them, they always cause more harm than good to themselves, and the world around them. If one is to possess strength, they must embark on a journey of self to understand what it means to them. Along the journey of self, an individual must challenge what they thought strength was and what it meant to possess it. Why? Because strength is a constant. Strength is something that all individuals seek to possess, but never know how to use. But it is by strength that we manifest what we believe to be true.

Strength is necessary for so many reasons. Strength is needed to make hard decisions for the good of all even if they do not know it. Strength is needed to maintain the peace that each person needs yet is unaware of. Strength is needed to bear the hard times and endure the struggles brought about by circumstances outside of our control that will challenge everything we hold dear. Strength is needed to fight for freedom, to fight against oppression, and to stand up for what is right when others are cowards. Strength is needed to be human. Strength is needed to be strong. Strength is needed if one is to do right by others when others do not know what is right for themselves. Strength is needed if one is willing to be true and be honest. Strength is needed to preserve the peace, maintain the balance needed to preserve and protect life. Strength is needed if one is to be the light in a world surrounded by darkness. Strength is needed if one is to fight for what they believe in, never knowing if all they do is for an absolute cause. Strength is needed if the future is to be brighter than we know it. Strength is needed if one is to be of high moral character. Strength is needed if one is to make sacrifices so that those who come after them may know a world better than those who came before them. Strength is needed if one is to live another day. Strength is needed if one is to be more than what they know to be true, something more, something better. Strength is needed if one is to break down and tear the establishments set by the old and usher in what is necessary for life to continue. Strength is needed to change the world. Strength is needed if one is to be their own individual. The greatest thing about strength is that we can become more because of it. The worst thing about strength is that we can lose everything if we become consumed by it.

Strength is needed, yet it is misunderstood.

CHAPTER 24

MORALITY

For countless generations, there have been numerous debates on what it means to be moral and ethical. These discussions are brought about by a focus on what it means to be human, what it means to be charitable, and what it means to be of a benevolent nature. Yet those who partake in these discussions can never reach a common consensus as morality is something too ambiguous to have one clear meaning or form of expression. Events such as war, famine, leadership, and perceptions seen through the eyes of the masses spark these philosophical debates. Sometimes it is the ignorance of one's human nature that makes them see morality in a way that others do not. And sometimes, it is the pursuit of enlightenment, the pursuit of human perfection that sparks the debate of morality. Yet there are different views on morality and what it means. Some see morality as a sign of weakness, a weapon to be used to assert and gain power over people, a way of life. The greatest problem of morality is that it is contradictory to our base human nature to be impulsive, irrational, savage, sadistic, and prone to responding based on only our five senses. It is basic human nature to kill, to desire more than what we need and have, to assert our power and dominance over others. It is human nature to spread life wherever we go yet deplete the land for what it has to offer. It is human nature to be greedy, to let our selfish nature consume us to the point where we consume everything around us until we feel full for the moment. Yet morality challenges that perspective. Morality is something that forces us to be the opposite of our basic human nature. Many shy away from morality because they can never be better because of it. Many shy away from morality because they believe they can never possess it. Some shy away from morality because it is too ambiguous and understanding its truths is an endeavor that will drive one past the boundaries of sanity. And some shy away from morality because they believe it makes them weak. Some see morality as the source of restraint. They see morality as a hinderance as it forces the one who wields it, possesses it to not utilize their strength, power, control, dominance, and influence over others to their fullest extent, or to rule those who are beneath them. Some see morality as something for the weak, as they pray and beg for mercy from those capable of ending what, in the eyes of their superior, is an inferior existence. Yet, some see morality as a necessity. In their view, it is essential to being human because it stops us from crossing a line that goes against the creation and preservation of life. Some see morality as a source of strength. Having power but knowing how and when to use it speaks to the integrity of the one who possesses it. Some see morality as a way to change the world. To some, it is am moral heart that is a giving heart. It is amoral heart that is a cheerful heart. It is a moral heart that is of a kind and gentle nature. Some see morality as the difference that separates the hero from the villain, good from evil, the defenders and protectors from the oppressors and evil doers. At its core, morality is tricky. It has no set interpretation, no set meaning. Yet when one looks back, they begin to see whether their understanding of it, and the form it takes, reveals if they truly are of an upright moral character. The irony of morality is that even though we don't know its true form and, the right means by which it should be expressed, in our heart's we know if we could do better.

———

What does it mean to be moral and to be ethical? Each human being struggles to do right by what they believe to be true with the means they have at their disposal. Yet we all fall short due to a lack of understanding of morality, or not enough time to walk in and embrace it for what it truly is. One of the hardest parts about living life is trying to live it the right way. Each person believes themselves to be right and others wrong, yet each person is slave to the understandings gained by having their own perspective. So, what does it mean to be moral? What does it mean to be ethical? What does it mean to be a good human being? Does being moral mean being equal? Does being moral mean being innocent? Does morality pertain to race, gender, creed, religious backgrounds and beliefs? Does morality mean something different to people of different walks of life? Does morality pertain to the rights an individual has as a person? Does morality pertain to gender, to one's social status? Does morality pertain to the amount of goods and resources a person has? Is morality different among the rich, the working class, the middle class, and the poor? Does it mean to be upright, to always tell the truth, to never lie? Does it mean to always give back to others, never to take from them what they did not grant us? Does being moral mean to always do the right thing because it is the right thing? Does being moral mean doing the right thing for the sake of being of a good character? Does it mean to uphold others, embrace others, protect others, and love others in a way that they should be? Does being moral mean being just?

But what do these things mean? What does it mean to be true, to be upright, to be just, to treat others in a way that uplifts them and does not hinder them? Is morality absolute? Are there certain actions that must not be taken to be moral? Are there certain guidelines that must be met to be considered moral? If we stay true to those actions that exist within the realm of morality, are we deemed moral? Is that all it takes to be moral, taking specific actions that others deem moral? Is morality then based on action? But where does morality start? Does it start with one's beliefs, one's way of life, one's decisions, one's goals, one's aspirations? Does it start with our thoughts? If we think good thoughts, positive thoughts, are we of good moral character? If we think of something that brings us peace and, joy, are we of a moral nature? Does morality then begin in one's mind? Is morality a spiritual thing or something tied to religion? Is morality something tied to the will of the divine? Is it even in human nature to be moral? Was it something created by other people to make them rise above their baser human instincts? Was morality something that was created to make people become more refined and sophisticated than their brutish nature? Or was morality a force housed within the human being that was always there? Was morality another aspect of what it meant to be human that came about when humanity questioned the reason why it did the things it did and the effect it would have on them afterward? Was morality something that was investigated when people began to believe that by expressing their baser instinct, they lost a part of them that made them whole? Is morality something we need if we are to keep or regain a part of our soul we lost or never had? Is morality something essential if human beings and humanity are to find their soul and be of a gentle, kind, giving, and benevolent heart? Is morality something needed if one is to understand what it means to preserve and protect others and stand up for what they believe in, yet do so in a way that does not demoralize them and make them lose their soul in the process? Can morality be a curse? Can morality be a gift? Can morality be a blessing? For in its essence, what is the use of morality?

What does it mean to be immoral? If being moral is to be upright, then what is the opposite of morality? What does it mean to be the opposite of upright? Does it mean to be untrue, malevolent, apathetic in one's thoughts, one's action, and one's heart? Does it mean that one does not care for the state of others? Does it mean that one is not charitable, of a giving nature, of a benevolent nature? Does the opposite of being moral mean that one does not care about what is right and what is wrong? Is an immoral person someone who does not believe in the traditional sense of right or wrong? Do their actions hinder instead of help others? Do all the things they do cause harm and despair around them? Is an immoral person an individual who is so lost that they do not seek to know the difference between right and wrong? Does such a person only think about themselves? Do they lack a heart, an ounce of mercy or forgiveness? Do they lack compassion, kindness, goodness? Do they lack the ability to empathize or sympathize with others? Does an immoral person seek only to destroy, only to hinder, only to decimate? Do they lack the ability to feel? Do they lack emotion? Do they lack the one component that makes them human, a spirit? Are they consumed by their negative emotions? Are they so consumed by their doubt, pain, grief, loss, strife, that they cannot see the light? Has such a person lost all hope? Have they lost all that they love? Have they given up faith? Have they given up on hope? Have they lost so much, sacrificed so much, endured so much that they have become numb? Have they become incapable of feeling something that was once so close to them, so dear to their heart, but is now foreign? Has an immoral person lost the ability to persevere, to hold onto all they deemed worth living? Has such a person been to the depths of their soul, their psyche, and accepted the darkness for what it is, have they finally cracked? Have they become so used to the abyss that they embrace it as the light? Has such a person known so much pain their whole life that pain is all they know? Is an immoral person a lonely person? Are they lonely in the sense that they had no one to comfort them, listen to them, care for them, sympathize with them, and empathize with them? Has such a person given up so much for others, but never been filled up with all they needed to the point where they have become empty, devoid of anything positive? Has such a person known so much pain their whole life that pain is all they know? Is the immoral person someone who is immoral at their core? Or have they lost their way to such a degree that their actions, their reasons, and their justifications are really a cry for help? Is it a cry for another who understands their pain to help them, and guide them back to a place they have long forgotten? Is the immoral individual just like all of us, except they embrace their darkness rather than, suppress it? Or is it that the immoral person is one who has accepted their inner darkness as the light? Can such a person be saved? Can such a person be redeemed? Is there hope for such an individual? Are they so far gone that they can never return to the moral character they once had? Once a person is void of all sense of morality, can they ever find their way back to be what is deemed to be moral?

At any given moment, there are countless faces in this world. There are endless names, too many to speak of, that show how many people walk the physical plane. And with each heart comes a story to tell. Each person has a mind of their own, experiences of their own. As they walk through life, they want to be respected, loved, and admired, and they seek to be benevolent to those who identify with them. At some point, each person comes across the topic of morality. Some glance at it and move on. Some stay with it for a while. Some dedicate their whole to understand what it is and how it shows one's true nature. And some people reject it and neglect it. For some, morality is spiritual. For some, morality is religious. For others, morality is personal. For others, morality is based on what they want it to be so that people may accept them for who they are. Yet deep down, we all wish to know in its absolute nature, what morality is.

Is morality understood by all people the same way? Do all people come to understand morality as something absolute? Do all people come to understand morality as something circumstantial? Is there only one way to express being moral? Is there only one way to express moral character in a physical form? What are the standards, rules, norms, customs, and boundaries that constitute a moral action? Who is the judge of what a moral action is? And can such action be acceptable to all people from all ways of life? Is there only one definition used to describe in its totality, the meaning of morality? Is there one meaning to morality that is agreeable to all people? Is there only one verbal expression that all people can agree is a moral one? Is there one written definition of morality that is agreeable to all people? Does it take experience to understand the meaning of morality? Does it take introspection to understand morality? Does it take a near-death experience? Does it take one being on their death-bed to understand the meaning of morality? If one is benevolent, do they understand morality? If one is generous, charitable, compassionate, kind, do they understand morality? If one is full of hate, malice, ill-will and intent, can they understand morality? Does each social group of people believe in the same type of morality? Does each fraternity, secret society, religion, organization with a creed believe in the same type of morality? Will people from all races, religious backgrounds, and all walks of life understand morality the same way? Will society ever come to understand the concept of morality? Or is it a bad thing that for as long as humanity has existed, morality could never be understood for what it is and what it means? Therefore, is

there hope for humanity if it chooses to understand morality in the subjective way that it does? And if humanity came to a common consensus,
would any good come from it?

How is morality expressed? By one's actions? Using one's intellect? By the
things we commit our lives to. By preserving, protecting the things we
hold dear? Is morality expressed by money, materialistic possessions? Is
morality expressed using goods, resources, capital, supply and demand?
Is morality expressed by giving back to one's community, one's nation? Is
morality expressed by duty, honor, and service to one's country? Is morality expressed by taking the life of those deemed the enemy by one's nation?
Is killing one for the sake of others an expression of moral character? Is
mercy killing or the killing of another so that they may be spared pain a
moral gesture? Is it possible to be moral, yet go outside the boundaries of
the law to seek justice? Is it possible to be a killer and take life because others deem it right, yet still be of moral character? How can one express a
moral nature, yet commit the very actions they deem immoral? Is morality expressed by staying true to one's principles, teachings, and doctrines?
Is morality expressed by being moral all the time and never deviating from
that standard, even if the present situation calls for immoral action? But
what if one were to stray from those principles, teachings, and doctrines?
Would such a person still be moral? If a person diverged from their moral
code to make a sacrifice so that those who live by that code could live,
would they still be moral?

Why is morality necessary?

At its core, what is the purpose of morality? In the end, we will never know.
But I believe that morality is necessary. If we are to be more than our baser,
impulsive, and savage instincts, we must be better. If we are to be upright,
honest, true, and better people, we must be moral. Morality is necessary in
that our actions have consequences. Morality is necessary in that what we
do will affect others. And it is up to us, the producers of our own actions,

to understand the importance, significance, and realistic implications of our actions. Within us is the capacity to do good. To do good by ourselves, our families, our friends. We can be a light to others, help others in different ways. Morality is important as it reveals to the individual who they truly are within. Morality reveals to us the extent of our hearts. It shows us our true character whether we accept it or not. Yet morality is that line we draw in the sand. It is the means by which we understand the boundaries of what we are willing to do, what we can do, what we will do, and what we will not do for the sake of others. For when we have morality, we are whole. Morality allows each person to tap into their emotional spectrum, to commit themselves to actions that reveal their true character. With morality, one understands that which could only be understood by each person individually... themselves. The pursuit of what is moral and what is immoral is one of the hardest journeys any individual will take. Yet when one understands morality, they understand themselves. When one understands their true nature, their true character, they understand themselves. They understand their beliefs, their core ideas, their reasons why, their justifications for those reasons, the true extent of their emotional connection to themselves and others. Morality is necessary because it allows each person to be whole, to understand what it means to be human, what it means to feel, to have emotion, or to have the capacity to empathize, sympathize with others. Morality is important because it allows us to tackle one of the hardest obstacles that lies in our way... our own moral nature, which is unknown to us. Morality allows each person to know where they stand when all they believe is put to question. Morality is necessary as it allows each person to know in what contexts they will exhibit a benevolent or malice behavior toward others.

Yet morality is something that all human beings possess, whether they know it or not. And one of the worst things any person can ever do is to neglect who they are within. The worst thing anyone can ever do is to give up on themselves and on others. But the greatest thing a person can ever do is to take the time and the journey to understand what truly lies within, The greatest thing a person can do is care, be of a good nature, a kind nature, of good character. The greatest thing one can achieve is to become better for that which they stand for, and to do right by others because of it.

CHAPTER 25

BALANCE

What surrounds the human being are three planes of existence: the mind, the body, and the spirit. Within the individual is the ability to interact with the material plane, the awareness of one's own existence by way of their conscious and subconscious inner life, and the yearnings of something that lies dormant within them yet goes deeper than what they physically interact with and consciously and subconsciously perceive. Within the human being is something complex yet intrinsic to our being. Within the human being is something contradictory yet essential to our nature. Within the human being is rationality and spirituality. Within the human being is irrationality and rationality. Within the human being is the spiritual nature and the mundane nature. Within the human being is the ability to create the materialistic and yet the yearning to comprehend and explore the essence of the source that is behind it. Within the human being is logic, yet emotion. Within the human being are great intellect, rationality, reasoning, and logical capabilities, yet the ability to have wisdom, understanding, insight at a level that goes deeper than what the mind knows. Within the human being is the ability to be detached from a situation, to see it in an objective manner. At the same time people have the ability to feel what they experience in a way that makes them feel alive, to have their own subjective experience. Within the human being is the ability to be savage, cold, brutish, selfish, sadistic, cruel, malevolent, primitive. Yet within us is the ability to be refined, sophisticated, moral, upright, conscious, caring, and compassionate, and to seek our higher being. Within the human being is a basic nature, a compulsive nature, an impulsive nature, an instinctual nature. Yet within us is a desire to become more than what we were born to be. While we are born with little to no understanding of the world, with time we can rise to be more than what the world has ever known.

It is no wonder that human beings are always singular yet diverse in their nature, and that humanity can be so basic in its nature yet vast in its capacity to create that which is greater than itself. As one begins to ponder their inward nature, they begin to understand that which lies within. Within them is something primal, yet something sophisticated. Within them is something raw and untapped, something unique, specific, and intimate only to them. Within them is that which can be perceived by others as of a foreign nature, yet it is something that is intrinsic to the one who possesses it, a reflection of their character. The individual who seeks that which lies within can begin to understand it as boundless, formless, shapeless, yet ever expanding. It can take a shape, form on the material plane, but its essence cannot house a physical form.

Yet the average human being does not dwell too much on what it is that is their composition. How does one understand the way in which to seek awareness and gain an understanding of the interaction of the mind, the body, the spirit, and all that comes with it? How does one come to understand when to feel and when to think? How does one come to know when to persevere, push forward, fight their way through by way of the body and spirit, and when to do so by way of their intellect? How does one walk by their higher being when they are slave to the desires and temptations of their physical form? How does one come to understand the logical, intellectual, reasoning capabilities of their mind, as well as the deep, intimate, individualistic, and subjective depths of their spirit? In other words, how does one find balance within themself?

As a concept, balance can take any shape, form, and definition the individual who ponders it wants it to take. Balance from within (in a spiritual sense) pertains to all people, though each person is different. Many possess the same qualities but to a different degree, and each possesses their own soul that makes the use of their qualities and the understanding of what they possess unique. Therefore, finding balance within oneself is not the same for everyone. Within the human being is the logical and the emotional, the logical and the spiritual. Each domain wars within an entity, two sides of the same coin wanting ambitiously to convey expression through one medium… the human body that exists in the physical plane. Like all things, balance from an objective standpoint is misunderstood because human beings are subjective and can only live by their own perspective. Within the human entity are two contradictory natures that make up a whole, the yin and yang to the soul. One cannot express itself without the other, and one cannot live without the other.

The mind interprets all that is around us in a manner known to and understood by all, yet it is the spirit that can go to a place that only the individual can go (if they are willing). For how does one find balance between the mind and the spirit? How does one connect the logical to the spiritual, and how does one express the spiritual through the logical? How does one interpret the essence of something that cannot be put into words or understood by logical doctrine, and how does one explain the essence of the spiritual in a way that all people will understand? Not only is there rationality and spirituality within the human being, there is emotion. How does one explain the emotional? How does one balance out their emotional and logical nature? How does one know when to feel, and how does one when to think? How does one know when to let the situation hit them to a point where they break down and allow primal instinct and action to take ahold of them, and how does one know when to think through the situation without being consumed by their emotions? How does one know when to be attached to the moment, to the situation in a way that allows them to feel from the heart? How does one know when to bask within their emotional nature? When the situation or the circumstances hit close to home? When the situation affects them or those close to them directly? When they align the situation with their moral values or what they deem to be moral or of a moral nature? But when does one know when to be logical in a situation? Does one rely on rationality when the situation affects others not close to them or does not affect them at all? Does one rely on rationality all the time to make sure that if they are to delve into their emotions, they have reasons and justifications for doing so? Does one choose to be rational over emotional because being rational speaks to a higher state of mind, or being a sophisticated human being, while being emotional speaks to being consumed by a primitive state of mind? When does one choose to be rational and not emotional? When does one choose to be emotional and not rational? When does one choose to be spiritual and not rational? When does one choose to be spiritual over being emotional? When does one choose to be rational over spiritual? And when does one choose to be emotional over being spiritual? Can a human being ever find a perfect balance between their emotions, their intellect, and their spiritual nature? Can such things exist in harmony in one entity? Can such expressions of the human being co-exist, be in harmony, and be embraced by one medium (the physical plane) while still being in one entity?

What is balance? What is balance of the inward nature? Is it the understanding of the mind, the body, the spirit, one's emotions as they affect the human body, the human soul, and the human psyche? Is it the unison of all these different components that make up the human being? Is it the harmony found between these components in a way that works together and not against the human being, putting them in a state of inner turmoil, a warring nature? Is balance understanding these components of the human being? So why do we speak of the balance of the soul if it is more than just the soul (but the mind, body, and emotions)? Is it because for so long, the common belief was that the spirit was and is the true essence of the individual, thus we must emphasize it more than anything else? Why do we speak of finding balance of the mind if it is more than just the mind (but the body, spirit, and one's emotions)? Is it that the mind is where the psyche is housed, where all that we perceive consciously and subconsciously is stored, thus we must find a means of seeking balance in the mind that we deem to be the spirit? How is this balance found among all these forms of expression of the human being? Is it found through meditation? Is it found through introspection? Is it found through philosophy? Is it found by deep pondering of our soul, our nature, our being as humans, and as individual people with our own existence? Is it done by accepting that which we are in so many ways? Is it found by accepting how different we are in the use of our mind and of our body and how these reflect our soul? Is it found by studying academic texts that speak in detail about the inward nature of the human soul? If each person is different, unique in their own way, how do they go about finding internal balance? How does a person understand themself, while trying to find inward balance of what they possess to the degree they possess it?

Each person is different. Each person has their own attributes, qualities, gifts, skills, talents, and traits, and each expresses them to various degrees. Yet very individual wants to amount to something different in their life. Some want to be influential thinkers; some want to be innovators; some want to be researchers; and, some want to be leaders, advocates, protectors and preservers. Each person wants to amount to what they deem to be the epitome of their human potential. Yet how does one find balance for themself if they are surrounded by those who seek something different? Even when they are amongst those with similar aspirations, they are still separated by those individuals by way of their beliefs and experiences, which either reinforce or hinder their aspirations. Yet how do they find balance within? Is balance spiritual to some and not to others? Is balance tied to religion for some and not for others? Is balance dependent on what profession one has? Or is balance merely a concept of how one handles multiple things at one time that pull them in opposite and sometimes contradictory directions? So, what is balance? Is it the full comprehension of the entirety of the human being? Is balance the comprehension of the human soul, leading a person to a better understanding of what they are internally and to an awareness of who they are or could be? Is balance just a concept that holds little meaning to people? Is balance just a concept that was created to describe to people a need to rely on more than one thing rather than putting all their eggs in one basket? Or is balance more than just a concept? Does it speak to the human being in a way that is misunderstood by all, yet crucial? Is there truth to balance as it pertains to humanity?

Why the need for balance?

Most people do not care about what lies within them, because they cannot see it. Most people care for only what they can hold, perceive, quantify, and calculate. The greatest downfall of all people is never taking the time to understand what they truly possess. In the modern era, we focus more on the future than we do the past. We put energy into the things created to make life on this earth better at the cost of our emotions, our spirituality, and our intellect. We focus so much more on the things outside ourselves that we never take the time to understand that which lies within. We call ourselves sophisticated, refined, of a higher intellect, and able to accomplish a multitude of tasks. Yet our understanding of ourselves is less than that of those who came before us and did more with, fewer resources.

In the modern era, man sacrificed his soul to advance his mind. Man would rather be a machine and be logical, than be a human and be logical, emotional, and spiritual. It seems that people would rather focus on the one thing they can understand and come together around than be unique, be themselves, and become the greatest they can be in mind, body, and spirit. Looking at the world around me, I see that people would rather be humans prone to logical error by way of their emotions, than being human and feeling with their hearts. It would seem that people today would rather hide from their own nature, as history has shown how illogical they can be when misguided by a wrong cause, so they could be better than their ancestors. Looking at this world, it would seem that people would rather give into their intellect because others can question it in a way they understand. But the journey of the soul, the quest of the heart, the voyage to know thyself is one they would steer clear of due to the loneliness they would face on such an existential quest.

People are many things, and stupid is one of them (probably in the top two). In an attempt to right the wrongs of the past, they turned from the doctrines of their ancestors with the belief that what was of the past was wrong and illogical. Yet when I look at their current works, mindsets, ways of thinking, reasons and forms of justifications, it is apparent to me that they are no better than those who came before them. The only difference is that they want to take a different path, and to be acknowledged for it while feeling good about themselves. While some turn to spirituality to understand the soul and all that lies within, some looked to the mind. Some rely on religion while others take to the realm of science. Which is right and which is wrong? Who is to say which will bear good fruit and which will bear bad fruit? Can history be the judge? Can the people who are affected by such things be the judge? What about the wars fought? What about the battles won? What about the lives claimed in the process? What about the leaders and revolutionaries these situations produced? What about the social, economic, political, religious, racial, ethic, and ethnical change these situations bring about? Which is right and which is wrong? Who is right and who is wrong? Is it the one who walks by faith and not by sight? Is it the one who walks by data, facts, proven statistics rather than just pure belief? Is it the one who looks to religion, or the one who looks to science? Is it the researcher, the scientist that is right or wrong? Is it the philosopher, the religious leader, the visionary that is right or wrong? Is it faith or logic? Is it reason or emotion that one should look to? Is it one or both? Or is it so much more?

So why the need for balance within the human being? The answer is simple… Because it is necessary. Within the human being is more than strength by way of the major muscle groups. Within the human being is more than just intellect, cognitive capabilities, reasoning, logical capabilities. Within the human being is more than just the emotional spectrum, which is to say that there is more than just one feeling we can get from being exposed to one or more situations. In the end, all these things: mind and emotions, make up what we call the soul. For some, the soul already exists, and the mind, body, and emotional depth of each person reflects that soul.

Balance is important because to achieve it, one must come to understand all that lies within themself. Therefore, balance is the understanding of the entirety and the depth of the human spirit. Yet balance is important in that it is the understanding of one's spirit. It is a shame to walk this earth and not understand who you are. It is a shame to walk this earth and not understand yourself on a psychological level, an emotional level, and a spiritual level. It is a shame that within each human being lies power, potential, and greatness that is unique and specific to them, yet they can never understand it because they can never understand themselves. It is a shame when a person has the ability, the capacity, to change the world for the greater good, yet lose themselves and allow themselves to be corrupted from something that was never part of them, but stemmed from something else. It is a shame how people reject their emotions for their intellect as they view their emotions as something weak and something that can be used to take advantage of them. Yet the mind is just as susceptible to manipulation, if not more, than one's emotions. It is a shame that people would rather be what others would tell them to be and live that way rather than look within themselves and become the epitome of their own character. To walk through life, to feel the greatness that lies within you, yet to reject the understanding that can come from the death of the soul. To live life seeing what one can become if they were to fully embrace their spiritual being, yet never tap into it, walk in it, and truthfully and openly embrace it because of the criticism of others is an internal death that leads to one's conscious demise.

Within us all is greatness, power, and potential. It lies dormant, it waits for us to tap into it, it yearns for us to explore its endless depths. It speaks to us in a way that it does not speak to others. It is special to us because it understands our point of view and agrees with our own perspective. And it knows us better than we know ourselves. It is as if it were ingrained in our DNA from our very birth. And there is a certain joy we feel, a certain level of fulfillment we achieve when we tap into this hidden strength we call our spirit. Yet to live life never wanting to know what that feels like, living life never seeking to understand it in our minds, emotions, and spirit is a life wasted. To sacrifice the depths of our being for the superficial happiness of material possessions and the pursuit of bodily pleasure fails in comparison to the needs of the heart (the soul). To sacrifice what we could be for things that will fade before we do, to sacrifice the understanding we could have and all that we could achieve for a mere moment of fame, prestige, and acceptance from the crowd is a life I could not stand to imagine. To live life never knowing what internal balance is within myself is a life I cannot say is worth living.

But why is balance necessary? When we come to know what we are, we know where we stand. When we come to know what we possess within, we know where we can go. Yet to know who we are and to know what we possess within ourselves in our entirety is something that is worth more than any physical thing we can possess. To have true knowledge of self is something that can guide us through the darkness in a way that very few things ever can. To have true knowledge of self means that nothing can appeal to our dark nature and overcome us. To have true knowledge of self is to have an understanding that goes beyond hate, anger, rage, our brutish/instinctual nature, but speaks to our higher being (in mind, body, emotion, and spirit). To understand how the mind affects the body, how the body affects the mind, how emotions cloud judgement, to know how our spiritual nature affects the use of all these elements is the core of knowledge of self. To possess such knowledge of the soul is the gateway to living one's life. When one attains such knowledge, nothing becomes an obstacle that blocks their path, and a door that can be opened without even having to open it.

For it is in this state that one has achieved balance. And when one has balance, what cannot be understood? And when one has understanding, what cannot be achieved?

CHAPTER 26

EMPATHY

s I live in this world, I find it hard to give back. I find it hard to give back to the many without the things they need to survive and live their life to the fullest. And as I try my best to give back, I see that what I am able to give is not enough to help those in need. For our wants and desires will always be more than the physical means to produce them, keeping us from realizing our achievements. As I live in this world, I try my best to give back to others, to show acts of kindness unseen to others but personal to me. Yet as I give, at times I do not want to. I do not want to because no matter how many times I give, it is never enough. It is never enough, and the more I give, the more others take from me. So why am I the only one I know who gives while others just walk about muddling in their own problems? I know I am not the only one, but sometimes it feels as though I am.

At times, I cut myself off from being the cheerful and benevolent giver I hope to be. But as I do, I feel dead on the inside. I feel dead knowing that even though I have so little to give, what is a little for me is a lot to someone else. And it hurts knowing that my stubbornness, my foolishness, my ignorance, and my anger prevents me from helping those in need. And the more I cut myself off from giving what little I can, the less human I feel. For in doing so, I cut myself off from feeling the pain others feel and the joy I get when I know I do the little I can to brighten somebody's day. At times I feel wrong for doing such a thing. I feel shameful, as my false sense of pride or my lack of understanding of what pride is makes me act so selfishly that I disregard the needs of others. Even though I give only what I can when I can, it still hurts to cut myself off from feeling such emotions. For all it takes is one bad day to see what the rest of us go through. Each day I try. I try my best to put some hope in this world. I try my best to put some faith in this world, some care in this world, some love in this world to remind me and those I come across that there are still some people who put themselves before others and who genuinely work towards a greater good. But at times, such a goal takes a heavy toll on the soul. It is not easy to hope in this world. It is not easy to be respectful to people. It is not easy to show kindness, gratitude, compassion, and love to someone you do not know. But it is almost as if you live your life every day surrounded by your enemy. Where is the love, and why is there is only hate? Why is it that we cannot get along with each other? Why do we have to constantly fight each other? And what exactly are we fighting for? Why can't we understand the other next to us? Why must we close ourselves off from our positive emotions and let the negativity from our hearts and the ways of the world influence our inner being? What happened to us as people? Were we born this way? Are we a product of our environment? Is this all we are good for, killing each other and leaving nothing but hatred for the next generation? Is this the only thing we know how to be amongst each other and within ourselves? What ever happened to understanding how the other person feels? What ever happened to trying to connect with the other person rather than just trying to dominate them and take over their will? Have we as humans lost such an ability as time has gone on? Is that something lost to the modern ages or is that something every generation has come to face on its own (just in a different way)? What did they call that ability, the ability to understand and deeply connect with another person? What do they call such a gift (if some consider it that)?

They call that empathy

But what is empathy? So many of us hear this word but we do not know what it means. So many of us have never heard of this word, yet when we do, we are shocked if or when we come to know its meaning. For what is empathy? And what does it mean to be empathetic? By definition, empathy is the ability to share and feel the emotions of another. It is different from sympathy, which is the ability to understand from an outside point of view what a person is going through or how they feel, but not necessarily know what they are going through inside or what they have been through. But empathy is the ability to know and understand what a person is going through because you yourself have been through it, have felt exactly what they are experiencing. But is that empathy in a nutshell, the ability to understand and share the feelings of another person? Are people the only species on this planet that can feel empathy? Can plants and, animals that have a lower level of intelligence than we humans feel empathy? If they can, what does that say about empathy as an emotion or a feeling all living things have? If not, is empathy something special only to human beings? But what does it means to be empathetic? Does it mean you know exactly what another person is going through or have an idea based on a logical and educated guess? Is it determining what their immediate situation allows them to feel in that moment, and ascertaining whether you are capable of feeling the same thing if you were in that situation?

But does sharing and understanding the feelings of another person mean that you share the same mindset? What good does that do for a person? How can understanding life in the trenches help the other person if you are also engulfed in the same flames they are, with no one to pull you both out? What good does being empathetic do if it messes up both people, who are too far gone to fully appreciate the connection they share? But is there more to being empathetic than meets the eye? Is empathy a thought process? Is empath an emotion? Or is it both? On which plane does empathy mostly occur…the emotional spectrum or the mental plane? Is empathy something that can be mentally or scientifically taught? Or is it something that can only be felt? Is empathy something innate to all human beings and walks of life? Or is it something that can be learned from our surroundings? I it something based on our social climate and the time period in which we live in? Is the empathy of today the same for everyone of this day and age? Is the standard of empathy the same for those who lived in ancient times? Does empathy mean what we believe it to be today, only for it to have meant something else many years ago? And if so, the standards of empathy change based on the society and period its principles are adopted in. How then do we know if we are the empathetic person or group of people our society would lead us to believe? Will we ever truly be empathetic? Will we ever be the pinnacle, the zenith, the epitome, the true ideal of empathy each person deems themselves to be? If so, how will that reflect itself onto us in the lives that we live? Will such an answer have a common consensus amongst the populace? Can such an answer be one that is universal for all people? If so, what would that look like and how would the world be different today? If not, can we ever reach a common consensus, but greater than that… a greater goal?

Empathy, is one of the rarest things in the world you will ever encounter. It is a quality that I compare to finding a diamond in the rough. Such a character trait truly distinguishes a person and elevates them to a higher level of understanding that very few aspire to achieve and fewer have actually achieved. I liken such an attribute to as very important piece of the soul. For many things make a soul whole, but empathy is one of the biggest things a person can obtain. For it is only when we have empathy and truly possess it that we truly change the world for the greater good. Not everyone has the ability to empathize with a heart and soul unknown to them. But what is empathy?

To be empathetic in a world full of pragmatic realism is no joke. In fact, it is probably one of the hardest things a person who is highly empathetic will ever go through. For empathy is not easy to obtain, not easy to possess, and not easy to embrace, nor is it easy to let it guide you down a path greater than you know. For in order to have empathy, you must first believe that such a thing exists and such a thing has power, and that such a thing can influence you and how you think and feel. But empathy is not the same thing for everybody. Not everyone can feel the same way. Not everyone can understand what someone is going through in their time of need or in their everyday life. Not everyone has the ability to connect with another human being because they can genuinely understand them on a deeper level. Not everyone can comfort someone in a way that few can because they genuinely know the pain the other feels from personal experience.

What is it like to be an empath in a pragmatic world? It is like being an idealist in a world where everyone has given up and no longer has the spirit or will to fight for their freedom or whatever they believe in. It is like being the only slave on the plantation. One who dreams about being free of their own volition and physically works to achieve it rather than just imagining it in their minds and not actually working towards that goal. It is like being the only soldier in the entire platoon or army who has the will to fight and run toward the enemy while others turn and run away. To be an empath is a very lonely thing, and such individuals truly are lonely. Not lonely in the sense that they are isolated from the rest of the world. They are lonely in that they can connect to others easily but others cannot easily connect to them. Yet what this individual possesses is the keys to the kingdom, the jewels of the crown, the pieces of wisdom that makes a wise king wise and a just ruler just. For those who truly possess the spirit of empathy possess the ability to read, embrace, and be one with the hearts and minds of those around them. They have the ability to take in the feelings and emotions of those they perceive as needy as if the state of mind were their own. In that respect, empaths can feel as others feel, think as others think, and understand others by way of a perspective that is unique to them. From that, they can bond with a person on a deeper level in a way only they can. And from there, they can help a person in a way that only that person needs to be helped so they can be the very best they can be. For what empaths have is a mind and a heart that can unify the whole world because they can, in a way deeper than others, understand all walks of life and all perspectives.

But the problem with being such a rarity in this world is that while you absorb so much from others, such content can negatively affect you as a person. The absorption of such foreign emotions, feelings, and content that are not your own can corrupt you. For when you absorb hate from others, it adds to your own. When you take in the pain of others, it becomes your own. When you take in the maliciousness of others, you are filled with that feeling the same as if it were your own. And from the absorption of such energy (or foreign information from the outside world), we lose touch with our own inner being and become what the ways of this world allow us to be. We lose the deeper connection within our inner beings as we take on and adopt a persona that is fueled by outside forces, which influences our inner world. And in that sense, empaths struggle with how they are and how the world wants them to be. They struggle with the thoughts, perspectives, opinions, ideas, and philosophies of this world and those of their own. In absorbing other people, we become them. And the more we absorb people's emotions, the more we lose touch with the inner essence of our being. But in seeing how other people see life the way they do, their perspective can lead us to be more optimistic or more pessimistic. Yet nine times out of ten, we see things from the more pessimistic view than the optimistic view. And why not? Who can blame a person for coming to grips with reality and seeing life for what they believe it to be? But with all that pessimism, we lose faith in the hope of a better tomorrow, a brighter future. In taking in all that negativity, we only become part of the problem that plagues the world. But why be empathetic? Why be optimistic? Why see the brighter side of things when there is nothing on the brighter side to look at? Why work towards something that you yourself may never get to see come to fruition in your lifetime? Why try to connect with someone who is not of your blood or means little to you? Why try to see things the way others do if, at the end of the day, you will only live life the way you yourself see things? Why try to get to know the person next to you a little bit more when doing so amounts to so little? What is the point of being empathetic in this world of realists and pragmatists? What good has empathy brought us? Has it put food on the table? Has it put clothes on our backs? Has it put a roof over our heads? Has it put any money in our pockets? What can empathy do for us that being critical, pragmatic, and realistic cannot? What does connecting with another person's emotions do better for us than analytically determining something with our mind? What benefit can being empathetic and caring about a person deeply enough to want to understand them on an emotional and psychological level do for us? How is it better than being critically inclined to make an assumption about someone and their circumstances based on the facts and our predetermination of them in that moment? What does empathy have over being critical? What does connecting with someone on a deep level have that's better than critically analyzing them in a detached manner? In a manner that does not allow us to take in anything negative from someone who we know nothing about? What we can we gather from all of this, what can being empathetic offer to a person that logic and critical thinking cannot? Why be empathetic if such a ability is a rarity and a person blessed with it cannot bring about the unification of others? Why bother to adopt such a unique perspective and deep connection with others if doing so puts us in harm's way? What good does it do to absorb another's negativity when it affects us more than it does them?

Why then would we have empathy towards another?

Why then should one be Empathetic?

To be honest, I don't know why. All I have is my opinion not a definitive answer. However, I believe that people should be empathetic. I believe that people should be empathetic because being doing so is better than being pessimistic. For no human progress gets made and no great change comes into existence without the understanding of multiple perspectives. I believe that we should be empathetic because without empathy, we would not have the unity we have today. Sure, there will always be those who do not see eye to eye with others, who fail to see life the way others do. Sure, there will be those who fail to see how thinking differently can enhance their life and well-being. And there will always be those who fail to see the folly of their ways and the limits of their way of life in relation to the bigger world around them. However, it is empathy that has led to the unity that we as people have today, and that has allowed us to better understand and live amongst each other than those who came before us.

While being empathetic is not the easiest thing to be, it does go a long way in the long run, it is just that we are not there to see it play out the way it actually happens, and it does not happen the way we thought it would. But there is no greater thing in this world than to connect not only to your soul, but the soul of others on a deeper level. To converse with other souls, to understand them, to see life the way they do, truly is a gift. For it can take us anywhere in this world, it can propel us as people to a place greater than what our ancestors knew, yet few strived for… the promised land. It is only when we take the time to talk to others and understand the way they feel that we understand how the ways of the world affect us all. It is only when we have empathy that we understand just what is wrong with us as people. It is only when we learn to be empathetic toward others that we learn more about ourselves. It is only when we learn to be empathetic toward others that we grow as a person.

In empathy, we learn to let go of our needs and focus on the needs of others. It is only when we become more empathetic that we learn to be more in tune with our emotions and the spiritual being within us. And as we do so we as humans reach a higher state of mind and understanding. And it is that level of wisdom and understanding that allows us to unlock the secrets of our true potential and be the idealistic person we thought we could never be. And it is from there that we change the world for the better. But it starts with us. If God gave us this gift, then it is up to us to seek it and utilize it if that is what we seek to do. If we choose to do nothing with this gift, to waste it, then we become no better than all the things that are wrong with the world. We allow them to go past us, corrupt us, control us, and keep us down. In being empathetic, we listen to the needs of the heart more clearly than how the world in all its multiple opinions will let us hear. For the heart knows what the heart wants. But the heart cannot wait forever. For it is only empathy (among other things) that can change the world for the greater good. But it is up to the soul willing to take up the burden that can be the spark that allows the necessary change to come forth. The change that will guide human-ity down the better path, toward the brighter tomorrow, and, have the promise of a glorious future for us and all those who come after us (For it is about them, not us.)

And all it starts with is showing a little bit of empathy.

Phillip Anderson was born in 1995 in Queens, New York. Phillip considers the pursuit of character, self-discovery, and living a spiritually fulfilling life most important to him, as well as family and friends. His hobbies include reading, writing, exercise, and playing with his Labrador retriever Rylee. If he isn't spending time doing these activities, he is either spending time with family and friends or working as a middle school Substitute Teacher positively impacting the minds of the future generation in his community.

Note: Phillip Anderson provides deep insight into the human emotional spectrum as well as giving a deep introspective analysis to the importance of such emotions and principles relative to the human being in his first book titled *The Needs of The Heart*.

www.ingramcontent.com/pod-product-compliance
Lightning Source LLC
Chambersburg PA
CBHW051958150726
47999CB00004B/1440